D0715392

7·99 II

The Arts 5-16

A Curriculum Framework

The Arts in Schools project was launched by the School Curriculum Development Committee in September 1985 and completed under the auspices of the National Curriculum Council in August 1989.

The central project team

Director
Dr Ken Robinson

Project Officers
Gillian Wills (1985-86)
Dave Allen (1985-88)
Jill Henderson (1986-89)
Phil Everitt (1988-89)

Information Officer
Mike Cahill (1986-89)

Administrator
Andrew Worsdale

The project team has produced three major publications in this series.

The Arts 5-16: A Curriculum Framework
Oliver & Boyd 1990   0 05 004579 2

The Arts 5-16: Practice and Innovation
Oliver & Boyd 1990   0 05 004580 6

The Arts 5-16: A Workpack for Teachers
Oliver & Boyd 1990   0 05 004581 4

Slide Sets   0 05 004587 3

The Arts 5-16

A Curriculum Framework

The Arts in Schools project team

Oliver & Boyd

All rights reserved: no part of this publication may be reproduced, stored in a retrieval system, or transmitted in any form or by any means, electronic, mechanical, photocopying, recording or otherwise, without either the prior written permission of the copyright owners or a licence permitting restricted copying issued by the Copyright Licensing Agency, 33-34 Alfred Place, London WC1E 7DP.

ISBN 0 05 004579 2

First published in 1990
by Oliver & Boyd
Longman Group plc
Longman House
Burnt Mill
Harlow
Essex CM20 2JE

Typeset by Presentation Solutions, Harrogate
in New Baskerville ITC (Linotron 300)
Printed in Great Britain by
Longman Resources Unit
62 Hallfield Road
Layerthorpe
York YO3 7XQ

Copyright © 1990
SCDC Publications

National Curriculum Council
15-17 New Street
York YO1 2RA

Photo acknowledgements

We are grateful to the following for permission to reproduce photographs – facing Chapter 1: Keith Thomson; facing Chapters 2 and 3: Sally and Richard Greenhill; facing Chapter 4: Brian Shuel; facing Chapter 5: Phillip Polglaze; facing Chapter 7: Val Wilmer.

We apologise for the fact that although every effort has been made to trace the copyright holder of the photo facing Chapter 6 this has not been possible.

Front and back covers
We are grateful to David Menday for permission to reproduce the second photo from the top on the front cover, and to Phil Everitt for all the other cover photos.

Contents

Acknowledgements

The Arts in Schools project involved extensive and intensive collaborations over four years between teachers, advisers, artists, pupils and administrators at all levels in the arts and in education. The project also involved partnerships with the Arts Council of Great Britain, the Crafts Council, National Foundation for Educational Research, the Calouste Gulbenkian Foundation and the regional arts associations with responsibility for each of the local areas involved. We have drawn deeply on the ideas and enthusiasms of all of these in developing these publications. We want to express particular thanks to the project co-ordinators in the eighteen partner local education authorities and to the teachers in the principal development groups; to the full-time support staff of the School Curriculum Development Committee and the National Curriculum Council, and to the project's national monitoring group. We list individuals' names in the Appendix.

Ken Robinson
Director

Preface

This publication is one of the results of the Arts in Schools project, a major curriculum initiative launched by the School Curriculum Development Committee in September 1985 and completed under the auspices of the National Curriculum Council in August 1989. The aim of the project was to give practical support to primary and secondary schools in improving provision for the arts in the education of all children and young people. The project was concerned with all of the arts – including music, dance, drama, visual and verbal arts – and with the whole compulsory school age-range from 5 to 16.

The project was stimulated by the response to the report of the national inquiry *The Arts in Schools: Principles, Practice and Provision* (Calouste Gulbenkian Foundation 1982). It was organised as a partnership with eighteen local education authorities (LEAs) and involved sustained work with over two hundred primary and secondary schools, their headteachers, teachers from all arts disciplines, LEA advisers and institutions of higher education. The project enjoyed close co-operation with the regional arts associations, professional arts associations, the Arts Council of Great Britain, the Crafts Council, and the National Foundation for Educational Research.

Through practical work in schools the project considered six main themes:

- the arts and the whole curriculum
- the content of arts teaching
- progression and continuity
- assessment and evaluation
- special educational needs
- the school and the community

Drawing on its extensive work in schools, the project has developed the following three main publications.

The Arts 5-16: A Curriculum Framework

Given the many pressures on time and resources, and the wide range of arts disciplines to consider, schools have repeatedly called for advice on the sorts of arts provision they might offer. This publication discusses the central issues for curriculum planning and assessment and offers a general framework of ideas for schools to consider in developing their own arts policies.

The Arts 5-16: Practice and Innovation

The teachers taking part in the project documented more than three hundred initiatives to enhance provision for the arts in the curriculum. This publication draws from this rich reservoir of experience to discuss and illustrate approaches to a range of practical issues from curriculum planning to improving continuity and meeting special educational needs. Each chapter summarises major issues, reviews relevant practical work, identifies the lessons of the project and offers practical guidelines for future development in teachers' own schools.

The Arts 5-16: A Workpack for Teachers

Curriculum development involves staff development. This workpack offers ideas, resources and suggestions for organising in-service workshops with staff in primary and secondary schools and for use in initial training courses. The workpack helps teachers to tackle issues raised in the project's other publications and to relate them to the development of a coherent arts policy for their own school. The pack is designed to meet a wide range of INSET needs including use by cross-phase LEA groups and by teachers from individual primary and secondary schools.

The publications of the Arts in Schools project are directed at all of those who shape and implement education in schools: teachers, headteachers, school governors, parents, teacher trainers, educational advisers, administrators and policy makers.

The project team began its work in September 1985. The Education Reform Act became law in August 1988, introducing the new vocabulary and expectations of the National Curriculum. In shaping these publications we have aimed to take account of this new context and to suggest ways in which schools can develop provision for the arts within and through the new statutory framework for the curriculum.

THE NEED FOR A FRAMEWORK

1. What provision should be made for the arts in primary and secondary schools and on what principles should it be based? Should all pupils work in a range of arts disciplines? If so, how broad a range should this be and why? How do the arts relate to other areas of the curriculum, including design, crafts, and media education? The Arts in Schools project supported over three hundred curriculum initiatives in primary, secondary and special schools throughout England and Wales. The aim was to give *practical* support to teachers in developing the arts in the curriculum. Effective curriculum development needs a guiding policy — a framework of principles and priorities.

2. Throughout the project's work in schools groups of teachers, headteachers, advisers and others debated fundamental questions about the purposes of arts education and the kinds of provision needed. Drawing on those debates and on the insights they generated, we have two main aims in this book. The first is to help school governing bodies, headteachers and parents to identify the essential roles of the arts in the curriculum and to agree on the necessary range of provision in their own schools. The second is to help teachers of the arts to fulfil these roles by developing appropriate courses of work and relevant approaches to teaching and assessment.

3. Within the terms of the 1986 and 1988 Education Acts every school is required to make and keep up to date a written statement about its curriculum. This should describe the aims and range of the curriculum and the balance between its different components, including the arts. The curriculum statements of most local education authorities include the arts and these are a valuable reference point for schools. But as a rule they do not cover the detailed issues of curriculum planning which schools have now to address. The National Curriculum provides a statutory framework for planning, but the

> foundation subject areas, together with religious education define the statutory minimum scope of the curriculum; other subjects and cross-curricular themes can and should figure in schemes of work covering the whole curriculum.

(DES 1989d)

4. Many primary and secondary schools have asked for a clear framework for planning for the arts in the curriculum. The framework offered here has been developed by the central team of the Arts in Schools project in consultation with the national networks of local co-ordinators and teachers' groups. It takes account of the major questions which emerged from our work in schools over three years and from a series of working conferences, courses and seminars that brought together teachers from a range of arts disciplines and from primary and secondary schools, plus teacher trainers and educational researchers, advisers and administrators, and professional artists. (We use the term 'artist' here and throughout these publications as a general term to mean practitioners in any art form.)

5. There is a growing body of writing and research in arts education and we have drawn gratefully on this in developing this framework. We have three reasons for producing a new formulation.

(a) Much of the existing writing and research is about single disciplines. Work in different disciplines tends to use different terms to describe similar ideas. These differences in terminology are an obstacle to coherent planning for the arts as a whole in the curriculum. A single framework offering a common terminology is a necessary basis for dialogue and co-operation between the various arts specialisms.

(b) Existing frameworks have been developed for different purposes or phases, e.g. for assessment, or course planning, or discussing methods of teaching. There is a pressing need for consistent principles to be applied across all of these areas of arts education. Too often, for example, the principles of arts teaching have been frustrated by inappropriate methods of assessment. A common framework is necessary for curriculum planning, for teaching and for assessment so as to improve the overall coherence of arts education.

(c) Teachers have emphasised the need for a framework which is accessible and practical and that takes specific account of the new circumstances in education created by the 1988 Education Reform Act and the National Curriculum. The ideas and terminology we present here have been developed through detailed work with teacher groups throughout the country. They have been welcomed as a direct and helpful way of tackling the day-to-day issues of contemporary practice. Our aim is to offer schools a map of entitlement for all pupils in the arts: a way of conceiving the range and depth of provision to be made in arts education and of judging their success in making it.

6. There are three general themes in our argument. The first is that the different arts disciplines have a number of common characteristics and should be planned for together as a generic part of the school curriculum. This idea has been gathering force in education over a number of years. It has been articulated in different ways by various influential writers, researchers and practitioners in arts education including Malcolm Ross, David Aspin, Peter Abbs, Robert Witkin and David Best. It was the central theme of the 1981 report from the Assessment of Performance Unit on Aesthetic Development (DES 1981). It was a keynote of the 1982 Gulbenkian report and of the work of the Arts in Schools project itself. This is not to argue against the specialist teaching of different disciplines, but for greater co-operation between teachers in the interests of a more coherent arts education for all pupils. *This calls for a different conception of the arts in many schools.*

7. The second theme is that the forms and media of different arts disciplines draw on different aspects of young people's intelligence and abilities. This has significant implications for the range of arts provision in school. We argue that there should be equal provision for a number of basic modes of understanding in the arts as a matter of fundamental educational entitlement. In due course in their passage through secondary school, young people should be offered co-ordinated opportunities to specialise in arts disciplines that best suit their interests and aptitudes. *This calls for a new balance of provision between the arts in schools.*

8. The third theme is that arts education should be seen within a general context of cultural education. The emphasis in arts teaching in all disciplines is often on promoting pupils' own creative work. We will argue that, for particular reasons, the best practice in primary as well as in secondary schools gives equal weight to developing young people's critical understanding of other people's work and their knowledge of different cultural practices and traditions. *This calls for a shift in the balance of work in many classrooms.*

9. In developing these themes, we offer a single framework for curriculum planning, teaching and assessment, in primary and secondary schools and in all arts disciplines. In Chapter One we outline the background to current concerns in arts education and identify the main questions that a school policy needs to address. In Chapter Two we look at changing conceptions of the arts and at necessary questions of definition. Chapter Three describes the main roles of the arts in the education of all pupils. In Chapter Four we identify the principles on which provision in primary and secondary schools should be based to fulfil these roles. Chapter Five discusses the need to achieve a new balance in the teaching of the arts, and identifies the essential ingredients of this approach. Chapter Six discusses the complexities of progression and development and identifies the main areas for pupil assessment. Chapter Seven draws together the main threads of our arguments as a basis for the future development of the arts in schools.

10. A school policy for the arts should be clearly related to the aims of the whole curriculum. The general aims of education in maintained schools are set down in law. The curriculum of a school satisfies the requirements of the 1988 Education Reform Act if it is 'balanced and broadly based' and:

(a) promotes the spiritual, moral, cultural, mental and physical development of pupils at the school and of society;
(b) prepares pupils for the opportunities, responsibilities and experiences of adult life.

In these terms, we can say immediately that a full and balanced arts education in schools is essential because:

- the processes of making in the arts provide all young people with fundamental ways of formulating and communicating their own ideas and feelings about the world in which they live;
- understanding existing work in the arts, in all forms, gives young people vivid access to the ideas, values and beliefs of other people and to some of the most penetrating achievements of human culture;
- through involvement in the arts young people can respond positively to the social world and contribute uniquely to the interplay of ideas and values which help to shape it.

None of this is possible without co-ordinated and sustained provision for the arts in schools. Our aim in offering this new framework is to give schools a sound basis for policy and practice on which they can establish the arts more firmly as a cornerstone of the whole curriculum.

Chapter one

ISSUES AND QUESTIONS

INTRODUCTION

11. Throughout the debates on the school curriculum of the last ten years, the importance of the arts has often been acknowledged, but rarely given detailed attention. In practice the arts have often been marginalised in schools by an assumption that they are less relevant to contemporary priorities than technological or scientific education. There is now a pressing need and a significant opportunity for schools to reorganise arts provision within an agreed policy for the whole curriculum. In this chapter we identify the major issues and questions that a school policy should address. We review some of the issues facing the arts in the curriculum as a whole and outline relevant developments within arts education and in the arts outside schools.

THE ARTS AND THE WHOLE CURRICULUM

12. The necessity of an adequate arts education for all pupils has been recognised in many reports and statements on the curriculum. So too has the need to make significant improvements in existing provision.

HMI, for example, has emphasised the importance of aesthetic and creative education as one of nine 'areas of learning and experience' (DES 1985b, p.17). As we will also argue,

> aesthetic and creative experience may occur in any part of the curriculum, but some subjects contribute particularly to the development of pupil's aesthetic awareness and understanding.... Art, crafts, design, some aspects of technology, music, drama and theatre arts, in particular, promote the development of the imagination and the creative use of media and materials.
>
> (ibid.)

The necessity of providing an adequate arts education to promote these and other areas has been emphasised by educators from a wide range of perspectives.*

The government's commitment to arts education has been clearly stated. In the parliamentary debate which followed the publication of the Gulbenkian report, *The Arts in Schools* (Calouste Gulbenkian Foundation 1982), the Government emphasised that:

* The boxes in the text contain information and ideas which supplement the main argument of the book.

the arts are not merely a desirable, but an essential component of the education offered in schools. This means not only fostering the talents of the artistically gifted — important as that is — but providing opportunities for all pupils... to participate in artistic activity and to learn about the arts.

(Hansard 1982, p.100)

13. The Government developed this view in *Better Schools* (DES 1985a), arguing that the curriculum from 5 to 16 should be based on the 'fundamental principles' of breadth, balance, relevance and differentiation. In fulfilling these principles, the primary school should introduce all pupils 'to a range of activities in the arts' (ibid., para. 61): in the first three years of the secondary school 'all pupils should study...music, art and drama, on a worthwhile scale', while in the fourth and fifth years, all pupils 'should continue to study elements drawn from the humanities and arts' (ibid., paras 67, 69). Art and music are foundation subjects in the National Curriculum. It has been emphasised that drama and dance should also form part of a balanced curriculum in the primary school and in the first three years of secondary education, and that opportunities in all of these disciplines should be available to pupils in the fourth and fifth years.

In a speech to the National Association for Education in the Arts (NAEA) in October 1987, Angela Rumbold, Minister of State for Education, emphasised the Government's commitment to all of the arts in schools including dance and drama. Arguing that the arts should be considered 'as a whole', she concluded the following.

A national curriculum which simply turned out children who had first-rate numeracy and scientific skills would not be one which any of us would want. And pupils, teachers and parents would rightly rebel against it if it ever came into being. It is education in the arts which makes a significant contribution to the way children develop their feelings and understand their emotions. It is this part of the curriculum which can play the most significant part in ensuring that children, when they leave schools and go out into adult life and employment, have developed emotionally....We are also quite clear that much work in the arts demands intellectual understanding of a very high order. Anyone who has tried to write a book, or score a piece of music, knows that well. Education in the arts also helps develop the creative sense — the kind of lateral and imaginative thinking which is so important in solving the complex problems of modern life. And because many aspects of them demand practical, physical skills of a very high order, it represents a useful training for many aspects of life where these skills are of value. In addition it encourages that kind of self-discipline and persistence in the pursuit of difficulties which are an important part of the development of character.

(NAEA 1987)

14. One of the difficulties for the arts in schools has been a narrow conception of aims and objectives in public debate on education. The 1988 Education Reform Act came at the end of over ten years of national debate on state education. The principal emphasis of the debate had been on the need to relate the curriculum closely to the needs of the economy. Some commentators saw in this a need to narrow the curriculum to those subjects with obvious vocational relevance, and to focus on the 'basic' skills of literacy and numeracy. From this point of view arts education might only seem important for those who want to get arts jobs. Increasingly it is recognised that for all of the purposes of education — social, economic, and personal — a broad-based curriculum is needed which develops the wide variety of pupils' aptitudes and abilities. Arts education has fundamental roles to play in this respect. The Gulbenkian report (Calouste Gulbenkian Foundation 1982, para.7) argued that the arts make essential contributions in six main areas of educational responsibility:

(a) in developing the full variety of children's intelligence;
(b) in developing the capacity for creative thought and action;
(c) in the education of feeling and sensibility;
(d) in the exploration of values;
(e) in understanding cultural change and differences;
(f) in developing physical and perceptual skills.

15. The report concluded, as HMI reports have done, that in too many schools provision for the arts is inadequate and needs urgent improvement. This conclusion has been borne out by the work of the Arts in Schools project. In our experience the arts tend not to be given appropriate time, status or resources to fulfil their roles in the curriculum. Sometimes this is due to a misconception that they are somehow less important than other areas of the curriculum. Consequently, poor provision is due in some schools more to lack of conviction than lack of resources. Often the range of arts provision is too narrow. Many schools provide for only two or three arts disciplines. As a result, young people have inadequate opportunities for personal achievement. Moreover, some teachers, particularly in primary schools, lack the necessary skills and confidence to teach the arts effectively. Often this is the result of inadequate training.

Following the publication of the Gulbenkian report, the National Foundation for Education Research (NFER) undertook a national survey of the arts in the initial training of primary school teachers. The survey showed that many students were qualifying as primary teachers with no significant training in the arts at all. Fewer than half of the graduate and post-graduate courses had compulsory elements in art, music, dance and drama (Cleave and Sharpe 1986).

16. These factors combine to create a 'cycle of constraint' (Calouste Gulbenkian Foundation 1982): where the arts are poorly provided for, pupils do not benefit from them as they should; consequently, other members of staff, parents and governors do not see their real value; as a result, they continue to be poorly provided for in the curriculum as a whole. Provision for the arts in many schools has been inadequate because of these general factors in curriculum planning. But there have also been difficulties within the field of arts education itself. These include problems of communication and co-ordination between the different arts subjects.

DEVELOPMENTS IN ARTS EDUCATION

17. Arts education is conventionally taken to include visual arts, music, drama, dance and verbal arts. Historically, these disciplines have developed separately in schools, using different concepts and terminologies, and with different levels of status and resourcing.

Dance

18. Dance is the least well established of the arts in schools. Traditionally it has been organised through PE departments in secondary schools and has been considered almost exclusively a girls' subject. In primary schools it has usually relied on the enthusiasms of individual teachers, often supplementing their teaching with BBC schools radio broadcasts of *Music and Movement* programmes.

> The development of dance within the PE curriculum is due to the influential work of Rudolf Laban. Fitting well with the principles of child-centred education, his theory of movement allowed the development of dance as the creative and expressive aspects of PE. The resulting curriculum model for PE emphasised a therapeutic role for dance, harmonising body and mind.

During the 1950s a division developed between educational and theatrical dance teachers. The advocates of educational dance argued that the strict conventions and disciplines of dance technique were inimical to children's personal development and that performance and dance production were unnecessary, even irrelevant. This view was opposed by the dance and ballet schools, where children were not encouraged to move spontaneously and where rigorous training was seen as the foundation of artistic achievement. In the 1960s and 1970s these opposing views gradually forged a new conception of dance in schools. Educationalists came to accept the need for dance technique and the value of planning and controlling expressive movement. Pupils were encouraged to make dances and to present them to others, and teachers in schools have come increasingly to argue for dance to be seen as part of the arts curriculum in schools.

19. In the theatrical dance world during this time there was a growing appreciation of improvisation and experimentation, which coincided with the evolution of British contemporary dance. During the past twenty-five years contemporary dance has become firmly established in this country and has provided young dance teachers with new models of practice. Dance companies have made significant progress in educational projects in schools and this has given a further impetus to dance as a subject in the curriculum. There has also been a rapid growth in the availability and take-up of examinations in dance. The main concerns of the examination syllabuses indicate the range of current interests in dance education:

- to promote an understanding of dance as an art form;
- to develop expertise in dance performance and composition;
- to develop an appreciation of dance through observation and discussion of dance both in and outside school.

20. Dance educators have made considerable progress in developing a coherent educational philosophy, but there are many difficulties still to face. The popularity of contemporary dance has been an important influence on the expansion of dance in schools. But this is a limited form, historically and culturally. Dance education should give pupils some understanding of the many forms and functions of dance in the world. The predominant image of dance as a girls' subject creates problems for teaching dance to boys and girls together, and also for recruiting men to teacher training in dance. Furthermore, there are very few courses which train specialist dance teachers. All of these factors have perpetuated the low status of dance in the curriculum.

Drama

21. Until the 1950s drama in schools was largely thought of in terms of the study and performance of plays and was usually taught as part of English. From early this century progressive teachers had encouraged the acting of texts in the classroom and the use of improvisation to explore their meanings. Some had also argued that these techniques could be used to enliven teaching and learning in all areas of the curriculum. During the 1950s these ideas took hold of teachers on a large scale. The publication in 1954 of *Child Drama* by Peter Slade marked a turning point in the development of drama in schools. Influenced by developments in child psychology and liberal educational philosophy, Slade and his followers argued, as Laban was doing at the same time for dance, that the real purpose of drama was to promote the personal growth of pupils through creative self-expression. Young children given only minimal help and direction by teachers generated their own distinctive dramatic forms — 'Child Drama' — which were different from theatre as understood by adults.

22. The teaching of acting technique and the study of texts were questioned on two counts: first because learning technique interrupted the 'spontaneity' and 'sincerity' of free expression, and second because learning about plays and theatre was potentially irrelevant to encouraging children to express their own ideas and feelings. The value of drama was as a medium of creative self-expression in which directions from the teacher should be kept to a minimum. The basic precepts of Child Drama were developed in various ways during the 1950s and 1960s.

> Significantly, these developments away from the art form in schools were strongly influenced by innovations in professional arts practice outside schools. New approaches in professional theatre to directing and acting and developments in improvisational and ensemble theatre all had successive effects on the theory and practice of classroom drama during the 1950s and 1960s. It was the influence of the Method school of acting, for example, that led to popular caricatures, which sometimes persist still, of improvised drama meaning being trees — one of many exercises within the Method.

23. For the first time drama began to be established in secondary schools as an independent discipline. Schools began to appoint specialist drama teachers and some created separate drama departments. The predominant emphasis in drama practice over the past fifteen years has been on the use of role play and group improvisation to explore social and moral issues. Many teachers emphasise the use of these processes in other subject areas and in personal and social education. There has been a continuing debate about the relationship between drama as a method of learning, and the study of texts, theatre and performances. Some teachers argue that theatre is irrelevant to 'drama' defined in terms of pupils' own exploratory work. Others base their work almost wholly on theatre studies.

> Teaching methods evolved considerably during the 1960s and 1970s as influential practitioners elaborated on the use of techniques of drama as a teaching method across the curriculum. The work of Gavin Bolton (1980)

and Dorothy Heathcote (Wagner 1979) was especially significant, and in particular their explorations of the techniques of teaching in role. Although these techniques draw on the forms and conventions of theatre, their emphasis has been on the use of drama as a method of exploring issues across the curriculum. Critics, notably David Hornbrook (1989), argue that this emphasis has detracted from the importance of drama as an arts discipline in its own right.

24. The recognition of drama in the National Curriculum has been widely welcomed; its inclusion as part of English has increased fears about its future as a separate discipline. This issue was recognised by the Cox committee (DES 1989b) which gave a prominent place to drama in the attainment targets and programmes of study for English, but which concluded that 'the inclusion of drama methods in English should not in any way replace drama as a subject for specialist study' (DES 1989b, para.8.3). The issues now facing drama teachers concern the status of drama in its own right, and the relationships between drama methods in general teaching, and the study and practice of theatre.

Visual arts **25.** Visual arts are the most securely established of the arts disciplines and have long been taught in all schools: in primary schools very often in association with craft, and in secondary schools with design. As with drama and dance, educational thought in visual arts in the 1950s and 1960s moved to an emphasis on encouraging children's own creative and expressive work. Just as Peter Slade was to argue for Child Drama, so Franz Cizek (Viola 1936) had promoted Child Art. This was argued to have its own aesthetic forms and qualities and to be as worthwhile artistically as the work of adults. Marion Richardson (1948) and others contributed to the theory and practice of Child Art by arguing for the use of simple, vivid materials — powder paints, thick brushes and so on — and the need for teachers not to impose adult techniques and standards on children. Herbert Read's (1945) influential work argued for the principles of art education to be applied throughout the curriculum, and helped considerably to consolidate the place of art in the education of all pupils.

26. In the 1970s and 1980s, art teachers have had to respond to many developments. Two central issues are: the relationship between art and design, in the secondary school especially, and the relationship between children's own expressive work and their critical understanding of the work of other people. Design has become a major area of development in the economy and is now coupled with technology in the National Curriculum. Design has become a prominent part of visual arts teaching in secondary schools and includes computer graphics, fashion and textile design and three-dimensional design. A key debate is the relationship between applied graphic and visual skills as in commercial and industrial design activities, and the expressive, conceptual processes of fine art. Some teachers have moved closer to the interests of design and technology and are keen to promote this relationship; others see this as an abandonment of the basic principles of art education as expressed by Read and others, and have pressed closer to the fine art traditions.

27. These issues in primary and secondary schools have their counterpart in art schools in higher education, and have consequent implications for teacher training. As in dance and drama, the emphasis on children's own creative work in the visual arts tended to replace the teaching of artistic traditions and critical appreciation. In the last five years however there has been a renewed interest in this area of art education, particularly through the work and influence of the Critical Studies in Art Education project (Taylor 1986).

> The Critical Studies in Art Education Project (CSAE) was directed by Rod Taylor and jointly funded by the Schools Council, the Crafts Council and the Arts Council. The project arose out of a concern that 'the emphasis on practical work in many schools had become so dominant that the contemplative aspects of art education had virtually disappeared' and that there had been 'a consequent reduction in the amount and variety of verbal communication in the art department' (Taylor 1986, p.xi). The aims of the project were to explore: the role and implementation of art history and critical studies in secondary schools and to link these to the use of external resources such as museums, galleries and art centres; the contribution which could be made within schools by visiting and resident artists and craftspeople, and by loans of collections of art and craft objects. Many of the principles and recommendations of the project have strongly influenced contemporary work in schools and the educational programmes of galleries and museums. Rod Taylor's own work as Art Adviser for Wigan and at the Drumcroon Education Art Centre is a continuing source of ideas and inspiration for these developments.

Music   28. In a review of the arts in schools, Robert Witkin (1974, p.118) commented:

> Of all the arts we have looked at in schools, music is apparently in the greatest difficulties. Despite a long and in places impressive tradition, it repeatedly fails to obtain a general hold on the musical development of the majority of pupils and is considered by many pupils to be irrelevant to anything that really concerns them.

Outside the classroom, school bands, orchestras and ensembles of many kinds have long made an enormous contribution to the culture of school and community life. Inevitably, opportunities for pupils to participate in these activities have been limited by perceived talent, numbers and facilities. By the mid-1970s music inside the classroom in secondary schools had often come to consist largely of the study of the lives of composers, appreciation of Western classical music and instrumentation, and selective instrumental tuition. In primary schools music consisted of classroom singing, and playing of percussion instruments and recorders. By 1979 music teachers saw themselves under fire for 'elitism in our professional practice...our narrow definitions of music confined to the Western classical tradition [and] the inadequacies of our intellectual framework and teaching methodology' (Swanwick 1979). During the past ten years music educators have reappraised many aspects of their work. This reappraisal was given particular impetus by music specialists' planning for the introduction of GCSE.

> In *Music, Mind and Education* (1989) Keith Swanwick offers a valuable and wide-ranging account of music education and its relationship with the curriculum as a whole. He argues for a broader cultural base for music in schools and that:
>
> > the major distinctive contribution to musical development made by ... schools and colleges ... lies in the abstraction and practical

exploration of clearly identified musical processes across a range of cultural 'for instances' essentially in musical criticism.

29. Partly as a result of this there is a new emphasis on the importance of practical music-making and composition alongside musical appreciation. It is now widely accepted that music education should give equal weight to the three aspects of listening, composing and performing. The conception of music has also broadened beyond that of the Western classical tradition to embrace all aspects of world music. These developments have been fuelled by technological innovations: practical music has been promoted by the availability of new instruments; the proliferation of recorded and broadcast music has brought new worlds of music within daily reach of the classroom. The central questions in music education now focus on content and on the role of the teacher in stimulating and sustaining pupil's own musical activity.

Verbal arts

30. Verbal arts is a relatively new conception. It refers to any art form which is principally concerned with words, whether written or spoken. There are three themes in current debates: the first concerns the relationship of English teaching to the arts and the relationship between creative writing and critical appreciation. The second is the growing interest in oracy. The third, which relates to the previous two, is the need to recognise different cultural practices in verbal arts, including those that are rooted in speech not writing.

31. Creative writing has been a particular feature of English teaching since the 1960s when it began to be widely valued as a form of self-expression. As in drama and dance, this interest was part of the general movement in child-centred education. During the late 1960s and 1970s research interest in English teaching began to centre on the social functions of language and on linguistics. Advocates of verbal arts are concerned that this emphasis takes teaching away from a key relationship with the arts.

Peter Abbs (1982, p.1) argues that:

the intrinsic concerns of English as a discipline are literary, expressive and aesthetic...for the best part of a century these concerns have been obscured....This was partly due to the fact that English emerged from classics and unconsciously absorbed many of the habits...of that subject. It was partly due to English being linked to literary criticism and the historical study of texts with the result that it became allied with the humanities and was seen, therefore, as being more akin to history or social studies than, say, dance or art. It was partly due to the demands of other disciplines which insisted that it was the task of English teachers simply to impart...the general skills of the language narrowly conceived.

In 1983 the Verbal Arts Association was formed to reassert the relationship of English with the arts, with a particular emphasis on encouraging pupils' own writing. A major premise was that the teaching of literature had long emphasised the study of texts over the development of pupils' own creative capabilities in language, that education seemingly valued the capacity to criticise literature more highly than the ability to produce it.

32. Verbal arts includes spoken as well as written language. The inclusion of *speaking and listening* as a separate profile component in the recommendations of the Cox committee on English 5-16 (DES 1989b) confirmed the increasing importance that is attached to oral communication. The value of talk, said the committee, as a means of promoting pupils' understanding and of evaluating their progress in all subjects is now widely accepted. The Government had already emphasised the need to reconsider traditional teaching techniques in order to encourage the development of oral skills (DES 1985a). Oral communication was subsequently made a central part of the assessment of many pupils through the introduction of GCSE. The Cox report specifically related 'the promotion of confident and articulate oral communication' to pupils' understanding and enjoyment of the arts' as patrons or practitioners' (DES 1989b). However, the relevance of oracy to the verbal arts goes well beyond the discussion and appreciation of literary forms. The concept of verbal arts helps to recognise that within many cultural groups, the arts are themselves rooted in oral rather than literary forms.

Looking for common ground

33. This brief review of the development of different arts disciplines in schools highlights some common preoccupations. These include:

- the relationship between pupils' own creative work and their understanding of the work of other people;
- the place of learning skills and techniques;
- the cultural context and content of arts education.

Historically in most disciplines the emphasis has tended at different times to be either on pupils' own creative work or on the development of critical understanding. Interestingly, the visual arts are currently moving towards an increased emphasis on 'critical studies', just when music education is emphasising the importance of pupils making their own music. It may be that these disciplines are moving to converge on common ground. The danger is that without common reference points to signal this opportunity, they will simply pass each other going in opposite directions.

34. During the last five years there has been a growing recognition of the existence of common ground, and of the benefits to pupils and staff alike of co-ordinated provision. In some primary schools, for example, named teachers are given responsibility for co-ordinating work in all of the arts. A growing number of secondary schools organise their arts courses within a single department or faculty. Developments in GCSE, Technical Vocational Education Initiative (TVEI) and modular curricula have encouraged links between arts teachers and between the arts and other areas of the curriculum. This new rapport has been illustrated by the work of the Arts in Schools project itself. Teachers of music, dance, drama, visual arts and verbal arts have worked closely together within the project to clarify relationships between their work and to take initiatives with shared benefits to them and to their pupils. This new mood has created opportunities to develop the arts in schools within the framework of a common policy.

DEVELOPMENTS IN THE ARTS

35. We have outlined above some of the issues facing the arts in the whole curriculum and some of those emerging from within arts education itself. Developments in the arts outside school are also

posing important challenges for the future. In many ways, as we have suggested, the arts in schools have always interacted with the arts in the culture of society at large. Contemporary innovations raise particular issues for curriculum planning, as outlined below.

- Developments in the technologies of the mass media have facilitated new forms of artistic expression: in video, film, photography, computer graphics, and electronic instruments. These are having a profound effect on the nature of contemporary arts practice and on how widely the arts are defined. The media have also created massive new audiences for the existing and traditional art forms. How should schools respond to these technological innovations and their implications for defining the arts in schools?

- There is increasing contact and interaction between cultures, in the schools themselves, and through the influence of the media, in social life in general. These interactions are vividly exemplified in the cross-fertilisation of artistic practices across cultural boundaries. How should schools respond to such cultural diversity in the arts?

- The arts are increasingly recognised as a highly significant sector of economic activity, and of social policy. Local authorities have begun to develop arts strategies as part of their corporate planning, and the arts figure increasingly in schemes for inner city and community regeneration. What account should schools take of these broader community issues in their planning for the arts?

- Education has become a priority for all the main arts funding agencies and an increasingly significant area of work for professional writers, musicians, visual artists and performing companies. The Arts Councils of Great Britain, Wales, Scotland and Northern Ireland have developed education policies and many of the regional arts associations in England have appointed officers with responsibility for policies and programmes of educational projects. The Crafts Council, British Film Institute and the Design Council each have their own education departments. What are the implications of these schemes for arts education in schools?

We develop several of these points in the next chapter as we look at ways of defining the arts.

ISSUES AND QUESTIONS

36. Against this background of rapid change in the curriculum, in arts education and in the arts in general, there are eight core questions which schools now need to address to develop a coherent programme of arts education for all pupils.

(a) What are the arts?
(b) What is distinctive about the arts?
(c) What are the differences between arts disciplines?
(d) What are the general roles of the arts in education?
(e) What are the roles of the different arts disciplines in education?
(f) What range of arts provision is necessary in the school curriculum?
(g) What should be included in the arts courses?
(h) How can pupils' progress and attainment in the arts be assessed?

37. We noted earlier the growing mood of co-operation among arts specialists, moving towards work within a common policy. The enthusiasm for this is sometimes tempered by a concern that the main outcome will be combined arts courses. Teachers worry that such courses may be used to reduce overall provision for the arts at the expense of specialist teaching and that this will lead to a fall in standards of achievement. We will return to these issues in Chapter Four. A common policy does not mean that the arts must always be taught together. The degree of combination will depend on many factors including resources, teachers' expertise and the aims of the collaboration. The aim of a common policy is to identify differences as well as similarities in the arts so as to allow a proper sophistication in curriculum planning, teaching and assessment.

SUMMARY

38. In this chapter we have argued that the importance of the arts in schools has often been acknowledged in curriculum statements but that provision for them is often inadequate because of misconceptions about their actual roles in education. The difficulties thus created for the arts in the whole curriculum have been compounded by problems of terminology and communication within arts education itself. There is now a growing recognition of common ground between arts teachers and this is illustrated by the increasing numbers of arts co-ordinators in primary schools and of arts faculties and combined arts initiatives in secondary schools. There is also a new agenda for arts education that is being generated by cultural and technological developments in the arts outside schools. These emphasise fundamental questions of definition and purpose for arts education. It is to these questions that we now turn.

Chapter two

WHAT ARE THE ARTS?

INTRODUCTION

39. In this chapter we consider how to define the arts. In doing so we introduce the main themes which underpin the framework for curriculum planning, teaching and assessment that we describe in the chapters that follow. Outside schools the need to define the arts may seldom arise. Inside schools, where the curriculum has to be planned and agreed, some definition of the arts and of their roles in education is essential. Are they subjects in the conventional sense? If so what are they about? What are the differences between the arts and what do they have in common? Defining the arts is difficult and controversial. What the arts are and what they are for have been understood differently at different times and in different cultural settings. In some cultures there is no equivalent term or conception at all; in others its meaning is not the same as in Western/European cultures. It is this dynamic and relative character of the arts which is at the heart of our argument for new approaches to the arts in education.

CHANGING CONCEPTIONS OF THE ARTS

40. What are the arts? The House of Commons Education, Science and Arts committee (1981-82, para. 2.1, p.24) adopted this definition from the US National Foundation for the Arts and Humanities:

> The term 'the arts' includes, but is not limited to, music (instrumental and vocal), dance, drama, folk arts, creative writing, architecture and allied fields, painting, sculpture, photography, graphic and craft arts, industrial design, costume and fashion design, motion pictures, television, radio, tape and sound recording, the arts related to presentation, performance, execution and exhibition of such major art forms, and the study and application of the arts to the human environment.

41. This is an impressive list which illustrates an important shift in understanding of the arts over the last twenty years or so to embrace activities which have a claim on all areas of social and working life. This in itself may suggest the need for an effective arts education in schools. But defining the arts with lists of examples can raise as many questions as it solves. In what ways are these all 'arts'? Are they all art forms in the same sense? Is there no difference between, say, design and poetry, music and fashion? If so, what is it? Some attempts at definition have tried to answer such questions by identifying the essential characteristics of all works of art. The problem is that there are often deep disagreements about whether some works of art are art at all. Others, which may not have been thought of as art when they were made, may come to be seen as art by other people at other times. In practice, judgements about the artistic status and qualities of individual works often involve different criteria and always involve personal values. These issues of artistic judgement and discrimination are important matters for arts education and we will come back to them.

42. Part of the difficulty of definition — and a matter of some significance for arts education — is that conceptions of the arts vary between cultures and, in Western/European cultures as least, have changed throughout history. The ancient world did not conceive of the arts, as the modern world commonly does, as a separate class of activities from practical, moral or political activities, but as a quality of achievement in many areas. The Latin *ars* and the Greek *techne* were applied not only to activities which we now think of as the fine arts and the crafts, but to many activities including logic, mathematics and the physical sciences. In contemporary European culture, the arts are usually conceived of more narrowly to mean specific sorts of 'creative' activities, including music, drama, dance, poetry, literature, painting, sculpture and architecture — and by extension the professions and industries which support artistic production, including arts management and administration. Within this conception of the arts it has become common to distinguish between the 'high arts' and 'popular culture' and between different arts disciplines. It has also been common, especially in education, to distinguish between arts and sciences. These distinctions have limited the range and standing of the arts in the curriculum.

'HIGH ARTS' AND 'POPULAR CULTURE'

43. The development of some forms of art in Western/European culture has been closely related to patronage. As a result definitions of the arts have tended to change according to the patrons of the day. If there had been an Arts Council at the end of the eighteenth century,

> it would have turned its attentions to preserving the approved arts of gardening, swordfighting, needlework and dancing, while letting such commonplace arts as novel writing and drama fend for themselves in the commercial market.
>
> (Pick 1986, p.11)

By the end of the nineteenth century the classifications of the arts had emerged that are now largely taken for granted in Western/European culture: fine art literature, dance, drama, music, poetry, sculpture and architecture. So too has a distinction between 'high' art, supported and approved by patronage, and 'low' art, supported by popular demand. This distinction has significant implications for the arts in schools. Are the high status, 'traditional' arts of, for example, opera, ballet, 'serious' music and theatre, which often have the support of public subsidy or private sponsorship, more important in educational terms than commercial theatre, fashion, popular music, film, television and popular publishing? If so, why, and in whose terms?

The distinction between high and low art illustrates well the cultural and historical differences in defining the arts. As John Pick (1986) argues, had the distinction between high and low art been made in the time of Elizabeth I, 'we should have put all our efforts into saving the high art of the Masque while ignoring the ordinary vulgarity of the plays'. Similarly, 'the art of juggling is state-supported as a high art in the Chinese People's Republic, and the arts of circus are state-supported as high arts in the USSR' (ibid.).

44. Film and television, and the other technologies of mass communication, raise many new issues for arts education. To begin with, they have created larger audiences for the arts of all sorts than at any time in history, and have also created new relationships with these audiences. There is now a whole sector of economic activity, sometimes called 'the cultural industries', which is concerned with the reproduction and distribution of the arts.

While in the nineteenth century, for example,

> only one person in the world could possess the original painting of *Sunflowers* by Van Gogh, millions can now buy copies of it: if only a minority could afford to attend a live performance of a concert...millions can buy the record.
>
> (Worpole 1989, p.5)

Equally,

> some 2.5 million people watched the English National Opera company's version of *The Mikado* on the television at Christmas in 1987, and plays by such important contemporary writers as Dennis Potter, Harold Pinter, Fay Weldon and others are often watched by up to 10 million viewers.
>
> (ibid.)

45. A recent study of the 'arts sector' in the United Kingdom estimated an annual turnover of £10 billion, amounting to 2.5 per cent of all spending on goods and services by UK residents and foreign buyers, and to direct employment of almost half a million people (Myerscough 1988). The majority of the population now gains most of its experience of the arts through the mass media of these cultural industries. What does this mean for arts education, and what relationships are implied with the developing field of media education?

46. Technology has done more than increase access to the arts. It has led to new forms of artistic practice. Film, video, photography, television, electronic instruments, computers and so on provide completely new media for artistic achievement. Work in these new media and its mass distribution through the cultural industries has presented serious challenges to the conventional distinctions between high art and popular art, as well as blurring the conventional boundaries between the art forms of Western/European culture. The revolution in communications has not only created new media for the arts; it has also increased the interaction between different cultures, many of which do not make the same distinctions between art forms to begin with.

Artists use the materials that are available. The development of photography in the nineteenth century revolutionised the recording of people, places and events. Visual artists were quick to explore the artistic potential of the new medium. It also spurred artists to explore the non-representational possibilities of painting and other 'traditional' art forms. As photography developed, critics debated whether a photograph could really be art. Walter Benjamin (1977) pointed out that this was not the point. The real question was not whether photography was art, but what it was that photography had done for the *established conception* of art.

DIFFERENT FORMS OF ART

47. In trying to describe the arts we should go beyond the boundaries of individual cultures to ask whether the kinds of skills, knowledge and experience that we group separately under the headings of dance, music, sculpture, painting, drama, poetry, literature and the graphic arts belong together in all contexts. In many parts of the world the integration of the arts and their roles in daily life is taken for granted. Artistic practices in many cultures challenge the conventional Western/European distinctions between art forms, and between the arts and daily life.

48. Kwesi Owusu (1986) illustrates some of the differences in approach in an analysis of Afro-Caribbean and Asian arts in Britain. There is in Western art, he argues, 'a central artistic concern for the creation of illusory space'. This requires

> artificial containment to separate it from real space. Frames and proscenium arches accomplish this containment. Galleries, museums and other institutional spaces separate visual art from performing art, books from films, music from poetry. African and Asian carvings and masquerades share the real space of the physical world. Masquerades, which combine visual and performing arts, occur in the streets, and carvings exhibit a living and immediate presence in real space. The physical and social landscape is the immediate canvas of creativity.
>
> (ibid.)

During an exhibition of work by Commonwealth artists at the Commonwealth Institute in London, a child asked the Ugandan artist Sanaa Gateja how he became an artist. 'He began to reply by saying that in his language there is no word for artist. Artists, he said, are simply skilled workers like other people' (Van Santen 1988).

John Blacking observes that amongst the Igbo of Nigeria,

> the nearest equivalent to a word for music is Egwu, but this also refers to the dance, theatre, poetry and costume that are combined in performance.... The Moroccan oral poet inhabits a region between speech types which is at the same time a region between worlds...the poetry is sung and is as much a musical and dramatic art as it is a literary one.
>
> (Blacking 1982)

ARTS AND SCIENCES

49. In addition to conventional distinctions between high art and popular culture and between different arts disciplines, a distinction is often taken for granted between the arts and sciences. Sometimes these are seen as opposites, even opponents. The sciences and technology tend to be associated with intellectual and practical achievements respectively, the arts with feelings, emotions and recreation. This apparent dichotomy between the arts and sciences is comparatively recent. Its roots lie in the intellectual revolutions in philosophy, mathematics and sciences which erupted in Europe during the seventeenth century and in the technological revolutions that followed during the eighteenth and nineteenth centuries. Progressively during this period science came to be associated with 'objective fact', and, through its impact on technology, with confronting the practicalities of the 'real' world. The arts by contrast became associated with less worldly concerns: with beauty, values, feelings and 'culture'.

50. New insights into the nature of human perception and intelligence, and developments in the philosophy of science and of the arts have begun to dissolve these dichotomies and to re-establish the relationships between artistic, scientific and other modes of understanding. The sciences have many characteristics that have come to be almost exclusively associated with the arts, and vice versa. The processes of scientific enquiry draw deeply on the scientist's powers of creativity and personal judgement. The progress of science, as Michael Polanyi (1969) has shown, has often been driven by unexpected, unsystematic leaps of individual imagination, by sudden illuminations in which a scientist may intuitively apprehend a solution before fully comprehending it. Scientists take deep aesthetic pleasure in the formal qualities of theoretical postulates and proofs.

> Harold Osborne (1985, p.88) notes that:
>
>> the leaders of the new sciences of cosmology and particle physics, which together with molecular biology have wrought a veritable Copernican revolution in the imaginative outlook of our age, have shown themselves highly sensitive to the inspirational and heuristic importance of intellectual beauty, a special kind of perfection.... Poincaré...claimed that new insights in mathematics... emerged from what he called the 'subliminal self' and that this was guided not only by intellectual consideration but much more by 'the feeling of mathematical beauty, of the harmony of numbers and forms of geometric elegance. It is a true aesthetic feeling which all mathematicians recognise...the useful combinations are precisely the most beautiful'... J.C. Polkinghorne, former Professor of Mathematical Physics in the University of Cambridge, wrote: 'It is a recognised technique in elementary particle physics to seek theories which are compact and mathematically beautiful in the expectation that they will then prove to be the ones realised in nature. This is a striking fact.'

Equally work in the arts shares some of the recognised characteristics of the sciences. If the arts require creative imagination and aesthetic judgement, they also call on painstaking discipline in the acquisition and application of skills, and intellectual rigour in the pursuit of formal and conceptual solutions. These affinities between different modes of understanding are significant both for the planning and the practice of education.

DEFINING THE ARTS

51. Given the range of historical and cultural attitudes to the arts, on what basis can they actually be defined? How can they be planned for in schools? We have indicated some of the difficulties of defining the arts by lists of examples, or by looking at the features of 'artistic' products. In developing a framework for the arts in education, we think it better to look in the first instance not at artistic products but at some of the *processes* involved in their making. The practice of the arts involves the creation of objects or events that express and represent ideas or perceptions. The arts emerge from the fundamental human capacity for making sense of experience by representing it in symbolic form. As we will argue in the next section, this includes processes which are *descriptive, creative, expressive* and *aesthetic*.

52. One of the central themes of studies in human intelligence is the extent to which we make sense of the world by representing our experiences through different symbolic forms to ourselves and to each other. Verbal language is the most obvious example of this process. The use of words to symbolise ideas and events is basic to human intelligence. The acquisition of language is intimately related to the development of thought. In learning a language children are not simply learning names for the objects they use and the people they know. They are absorbing the patterns of ideas and understanding which are inherent in the vocabulary and structure of their language, the ways of understanding the world which their language will express. In learning to speak children are learning ways of thinking. There are two corollaries to this conception of human understanding.

53. The first is that human intelligence is inherently creative. We *make* sense of the world quite literally . We do not see the world 'just as it is'; our perceptions are filtered through the frameworks of ideas, values and beliefs that we have available to give them meaning. How we see events is deeply affected by the ideas and values we bring to them, and these vary between individuals, cultural groups and historical periods. Consequently, the correspondence between 'what people really think exists and what really does exist' (Kelly 1963) is constantly changing. History is marked by the often profound shifts of consciousness, in ways of seeing the world, which come about through the constant friction of ideas and circumstances *between* science, religion, morality, politics — and the arts. Human understanding is a process of 'successive approximations'. To make sense of events we 'thread them through' with ideas, and to make sense of ideas we must point them at events. This is the basic process of the creative mind, 'testing new ideas in the successive interpretation and re-interpretation of experience' (ibid.). It is essentially the same process in all modes of understanding, in science, and in the arts.

54. The second corollary is that human intelligence is multifaceted and embraces a number of distinctive *modes of understanding*. Our experiences are of many kinds and qualities and we use a wide variety of ways to make sense of them. Verbal language enables us to formulate some ideas but not others. There are some thoughts for which there are, literally, no words. For these we use other modes of understanding such as mathematics or music, or visual images. Mathematics is not simply another way of expressing ideas which could be put equally well into words. It is a distinctive mode of understanding that makes possible ideas and perceptions which are not possible otherwise, that without mathematics would be literally inconceivable. The same is true of the different modes of understanding of the arts.

55. We think about our experiences in many of the ways in which we have them: aurally, visually, and so on. The painter is not creating pictures of ideas that would be better expressed in mathematics. He or she is using a visual intelligence to formulate visual perceptions and ideas. Similarly the musician, poet, dramatist, dancer and so on use sounds, words, movement to formulate ideas which are only fully intelligible in those modes of understanding. We noted above that some cultures do not distinguish as Europeans have done between separate disciplines and that a good deal of arts practice in Western/ European cultures also challenges these distinctions. For this reason it is inappropriate to relate a definition of the arts — or a plan for the arts in schools — to a conception of artistic disciplines which is specific to particular cultures. A general definition of the arts needs to be built on a broader base. We have defined the arts as modes of understanding. More accurately, they draw from a number of different modes of understanding which give rise in different cultures to a wide variety of different artistic forms and disciplines. These modes include:

- the *visual* mode — using light, colour and images;
- the *aural* mode — using sounds and rhythms;
- the *kinaesthetic* mode — using bodily movement;
- the *verbal* mode — using words;
- the *enactive* mode — using imagined roles.

56. These elemental modes of understanding generate different artistic forms and disciplines within different cultures. The verbal mode, for example, may include spoken and written language. Speech is a feature of all cultures; writing is not. The structure and organisation of different languages generate different forms of verbal art in speech and writing. The enactive mode uses the capacity to represent experience through gesture and role play that is a pervasive feature of childhood play and adult life long before it evolves into formal theatre. Most forms of dance combine aural, visual and kinaesthetic modes in various ways. In Western/European cultures drama combines enactive and verbal modes — mime, for example, concentrates on the enactive and kinaesthetic. We will return to this classification in Chapter Four when considering the range of arts provisions needed in curriculum.

Within the Western/European tradition, schools of artists such as the Futurists, Dadaists, Surrealists and the Bauhaus have worked across a range of media. The work of the Bauhaus included crafts, design, architecture, painting, printmaking, ballet, typography, pantomime and literature. Many visual artists have collaborated with the performing arts: dance companies have devised collaborations with visual artists, musicians and writers; and musicians have developed distinctive forms of dance theatre.

WHAT ARE THE ARTS ABOUT?

57. The arts are ways of formulating and expressing ideas and perceptions of the world. They are not definable in terms of distinctive content or subject matter. An individual work of art, as Louis Arnaud Reid (1969) noted, may be about anything whatever that happens to interest an artist — just as a scientific investigation may be about anything that interests a scientist. In this and other respects artists and scientists have much in common: indeed there are individuals who are both artist and scientist. There are, however, some essential differences between the two approaches. Science is concerned with the development and systematic organisation of propositional knowledge. The practice of science involves observing specific rules and procedures of inquiry and verification.

This is not to say that the rules and procedures of science are absolute and unchanging. As Popper (1969), Kuhn (1970) and others have shown the progress of science has been marked by profound shifts in the basic precepts of scientific understanding — for example, from Ptolemy to Copernicus, Newton to Einstein.

The arts on the other hand are concerned with many different ways of knowing the world and range outside those of propositional knowledge. In the arts there are no universally accepted rules of practice and validation. Artistic forms and conventions vary between cultures as well as over time. In some cultures there are strict conventions of symbolism and technique — as in classical Indian dance and Chinese opera — but these are specific to those traditions. It is partly for this reason that understanding works of art, and whether they are works of art at all, requires some knowledge of the cultural context in which they were made. Acquiring such knowledge is an essential aspect of arts education.

58. The arts take many forms and operate within many different codes and conventions because they are concerned not only with what we perceive in the world but with the *qualities* of human perceptions: with *how* we experience the world. In some contexts the arts *are* the experience. Participating in dance, music and song is often the means by which a community creates and celebrates its identity as a group. In other contexts the artist works alone to develop unique forms to express personal perceptions or understanding. The arts include processes that are descriptive, creative, expressive, and aesthetic. Different theories of the arts have tended to emphasise one or more of these against the others. We see all of them as fundamental to the place of the arts in schools.

Descriptive 59. The arts are vivid ways of observing and describing experience. In some cases this is obvious, as in representational painting or the narrative forms of novels, poetry, dance and drama. They are also descriptive in the less obvious cases of, for example, abstract art, music, and lyric poetry. These descriptions are not necessarily of events, though they may relate to them, but of ideas and perceptions. To communicate through the arts is 'to convey an experience to others in such a form that the experience is actively re-created... actively lived through by those to whom it is offered' (Williams 1971, p.51).

Creative **60.** Artists are creative in the obvious sense of making things that did not exist before: a play, a composition, an object, a dance. They may also be creative in the more profound sense of generating new ways of seeing. Creativity is possible in all modes of understanding: in science, history, philosophy, mathematics and so on. The creative artist 'is an observer whose brain works in new ways making it possible to convey information about matters that were not a subject for communication before' (Young 1951). The discoveries of the artist and the scientist are exactly alike in this respect. Artists 'have discovered new aspects of space with one symbolism just as physicists have with another' (ibid.). In all cases the creative process of the arts involves developing forms of expression which capture and in some sense embody the artist's perceptions. This is not a matter of identifying an idea and then finding a form in which to express it. It is through developing the dance, the image, the sounds that the perception becomes clear. The meaning is uniquely available in that form.

> The process of creativity can operate at many different levels and within different degrees of freedom and constraint, according to the individual artist and the cultural context of his or her work. In some settings the role of the artist is to express prevailing cultural values within strict conventions of expression, as for example, in European or Indian court and religious painting and music. In others, as in the Modernist movements of the early twentieth century, artists sought to break the mould of traditional concepts of art. Picasso's *Demoiselles d'Avignon* was a famous fracture in the tradition of European painting which challenged many accepted conventions of pictorial representation, leading to the development of Cubism and new conceptions in visual art. The relationships between form and content and between creativity and convention are important themes for arts education to which we will return later.

Expressive **61.** The arts are processes of expression which may draw deeply on an artist's feelings about the subject in hand. Because of this, it is sometimes assumed that the arts are outpourings of emotion and non-intellectual. This view is based on misconceptions about expression in the arts. Expressive activity reflects an inner state of feeling. Not all expression is deliberate. A cry of pain is an involuntary expression; artistic activity is not. Involuntary and deliberate expression can be distinguished as expressive *behaviour* and expressive *action*. The arts are processes of expressive action. Not all expressive action is artistic. Some expressive actions are symptoms of feelings and are intended to give them relief. In the expressive action of the arts, the intention is not to give vent to feelings but to give them meaning.

Aesthetic **62.** The terms artistic and aesthetic are sometimes confused. Aesthetic awareness is a sensitivity to the formal qualities of objects or events. In responding aesthetically we are aware of such qualities as rhythm, harmony, balance, tone and texture. Aesthetic perception is not always positive, it includes perceptions of ugliness, for example, as well as of beauty. Like creativity, aesthetic perception is possible in all areas of human activity. Anything can be an object of aesthetic response: natural objects — flowers, landscapes, water — and made objects of all sorts. Mathematical equations and theoretical proofs can have aesthetic appeal in one sphere, just as accomplished performances in sport can in another. Aesthetic perception is an essential part of artistic perception, but these are not synonymous. An important difference between natural phenomena and works of art is that sunsets, for example, do not have intentions, whereas artists do. Artistic perception includes some grasp of the meanings of a work, of which its aesthetic qualities are part. Artists work within or against different cultural styles and conventions. A full grasp of a work's artistic qualities therefore requires some understanding of these conventions.

> A European seeing Peking Opera for the first time may have aesthetic responses to the sights and sounds it presents. But relevant artistic judgements are difficult without some grasp of the conventions and traditions within which the performance is made. European observers will have some conception of theatrical performance and of opera and may judge the work in those terms. Their aesthetic responses will also be influenced by the values and attitudes they bring to it, but these may not apply to the performance in its own terms. Similarly, a person watching Western contemporary dance for the first time with no knowledge of its styles and assumptions may have an aesthetic response, but is unlikely to fully understand its artistic qualities and meanings.
>
> David Best (1984) makes the same point.
>
>> Some years ago I was privileged to attend a performance by Ram Gopal, the great Indian classical dancer. I was captivated by the superb quality of his performance, yet I was quite unable to understand it since I knew nothing of the significance of, for instance, the range of subtle and intricate hand gestures, each with precise meaning, characteristic of this mode of dance. It is clear that my appreciation was aesthetic not artistic.

THE ARTS AND THE SOCIAL CULTURE

63. Since the nineteenth century, the term culture has often been used to mean the arts. This is misleading. Increasingly it is used now to mean a society's whole way of life: its political and economic structures, its social and working relations, its patterns of belief, philosophical ideas, moral values and so on. Each of these various aspects of the social culture interacts with the other to give different societies and groups their distinctive character and dynamic. The roles of the arts vary widely between cultural groups. In some societies and at some times the artist is an iconoclast who challenges prevailing attitudes and values, generating new perceptions to challenge established ways of thinking. At others, artists are the 'voice of the community', shaping images and artefacts to give form to a community's deepest values and convictions. In all cases, artists interact with the social culture: using the materials and technologies it generates; addressing the ideas and values it holds; working within or against the artistic and aesthetic conventions it recognises. It is for these reasons that the forms and conventions of arts practice can vary so markedly between cultural groups and periods.

SUMMARY

64. In this chapter we have looked at some of the problems involved in defining the arts, and have questioned some common distinctions made between high art and popular culture, between arts disciplines, and between arts and sciences. We have argued that the arts should be seen as modes of understanding which reflect the basic human capacity to make sense of experience through the use of different symbolic forms. We have outlined some of the processes involved and their significance for individual development and for the social culture. From this perspective, as we argue in the next chapter, a balanced arts education fulfils a number of fundamental roles in the curriculum of all children and young people.

Chapter three

THE ARTS AND EDUCATION

INTRODUCTION

65. In this chapter we outline the main roles of the arts in education. A policy for the arts in schools should say what the arts contribute to the education of all pupils within the aims of the curriculum as a whole. The 1988 Education Reform Act is related to the six general aims of education that were distilled in *Better Schools* (DES 1985a) from the curriculum statements of schools and local education authorities. These aims are to help pupils to:

(a) develop lively, enquiring minds, the ability to question and argue rationally and to apply themselves to tasks and physical skills;

(b) acquire understanding, knowledge and skills relevant to adult life and employment in a fast changing world;

(c) use language and number effectively;

(d) develop personal moral values, respect for religious values, and tolerance of other races, religions and ways of life;

(e) understand the world in which they live, and the interdependence of individuals, groups and nations;

(f) appreciate human achievements and aspirations.

(DES 1985a, para.44)

An effective arts education is essential to the realisation of most of these aims. The arts are modes of understanding which penetrate and interact with many areas of individual and cultural life. As such they are essential elements of what we will call here *cultural* education.

THE ARTS AND CULTURAL EDUCATION

66. Schools are concerned with the development of all pupils as unique individuals. As we noted in Chapter One, in the arts — as in other areas of the curriculum — this concern led for a time to an emphasis on encouraging pupils to express their own feelings as freely as possible, an emphasis that was often in preference to encouraging an understanding of the work of other people. This was also seen as a valuable counterbalance to an emphasis in other areas of the curriculum on factual learning. There are several difficulties in this view of arts education.

67. Laying the emphasis on the expression of feelings and emotions can imply that the arts are not involved in intellectual development. The arts are concerned with feelings, but they are also deeply enmeshed in ideas and intellectual enquiry — indeed, they extend the very idea of intellectual ability. So far from separating intellect and feeling, work in the arts illustrates the intimate ways in which they are bound together. The emphasis on self-expression may also lead to a disregard of the cultural dimension of individual development. Young people do not develop their ideas and values on their own in 'isolated bubbles of originality' (Abbs 1988), but rather they absorb many of them from the cultural groups and communities to which they belong. Children are born into a culture, and for as long as they live in it they are under pressure to live by it,

> to see the world according to this set of values rather than that, and to behave in these ways rather than those. Consciously and unconsciously they absorb and reflect their culture through the people they meet, the clothes they wear, the music they listen to and the stories they tell.
>
> (Calouste Gulbenkian Foundation 1982, p.38)

68. Cultural differences in language, dress and behaviour often reflect profound differences in ways of seeing and making sense of the world. Events that may be 'steeped in significance within one culture may have no significance within another' (ibid. p.37). Consequently, developing individuality through free self-expression can be self-defeating. Children's 'free expressive' work in art, drama, dance and so on does not consist wholly of unique childhood visions. It is often heavily influenced in content and style by the dominant cultural ideas and conventions to which those children are exposed. Without the challenge and rigour of genuine creative enquiry, young people may simply be expressing 'ideas they have inherited and emotions they have been taught to feel' (Polanyi 1969). An education concerned with individuality should enable young people to take an enquiring attitude to their own ideas and values and to those that surround them. Individual development, that is, should be set in a context of cultural education.

69. For over twenty years there has been a growing awareness of the need for education to take full account of the increasing diversity of British culture, and the increasing interaction between world cultures. 'Multicultural' education gives rise to complex issues for schools, related to the different cultural communities they serve. These issues have been the subject of sustained debate — most recently and in most detail in the Swann report (DES 1985c) — and there have been many thoughtful and creative initiatives in schools to tackle them. Some examples from the Arts in Schools project are described in our related publication *The Arts 5-16: Practice and Innovation.* Our conception of cultural education relates in many ways to that of multicultural education. It is however a more general term and we see some advantage in this.

70. Multicultural education is sometimes seen as teaching pupils about *other* cultures. One shortcoming of this approach is that it may leave pupils' own cultural assumptions unexamined while they are invited to survey a variety of 'foreign' cultures. A second and consequent difficulty is the risk of superficiality from short projects and courses that sample different cultures. These difficulties arise when multicultural education is seen as something separate from teaching the 'mainstream' culture, whose values and perspectives are left unquestioned. An effective multicultural education in schools must emphasise the central importance of pupils analysing and comparing their own cultures in relation to others. Cultural education in this fundamental sense embraces the key principles of multicultural education. It is one which:

- helps young people to recognise and analyse their own cultural values and assumptions;
- brings them into contact with the attitudes, values and institutions of other cultures;
- enables them to relate contemporary values to the historical forces which moulded them;
- alerts them to the evolutionary nature of culture and to the potential for change.

71. The six aims that underpin the 1988 Education Reform Act (see p.29) stress in different terms the central importance of each of these objectives. Achieving them through arts education certainly means involving young people in the creative practice of the arts. It also involves bringing their own work into a dynamic and creative relationship with the work of other people. In terms of the issues of definition discussed in the last chapter and those of educational principles outlined here, it follows that arts education should not be confined to the practices and conventions of Western/European cultures, but that it should of necessity:

- extend pupils' cultural experiences by drawing on forms and styles of work from beyond Western/European cultures;
- explore the influences of non-Western forms on Western arts, and vice versa.

72. In the practice of the arts young people can be enabled to clarify and communicate their own ideas and values. Through critical engagement with existing work they can be brought into vivid contact with the ideas, values and sensibilities of other people in their own and in other cultural communities. Working in and learning about the arts are essential and mutually enriching elements of cultural education. Just as in other modes of understanding, 'the arts thrive best not in private culs-de-sac but at the busy crossroads of symbolic life' (Abbs 1988).

THE ROLES OF ARTS EDUCATION

73. Within this general conception of cultural education the arts fulfil a number of specific and essential roles in schools: in intellectual and aesthetic development; in the education of feeling; in the exploration of values, in personal and social education.

Intellectual development

74. Since the seventeenth century the dominant conception of human intelligence has been based on the capacity for deductive reasoning and for acquiring propositional knowledge. These have been the foundation of academic education since the beginning of compulsory schooling. All children have these capacities to varying extents and it is part of the job of education to develop them as fully as possible. However, human intelligence is richer and more varied than the

possession of these capacities alone. It includes many different modes of understanding, including those that give rise to the arts. An effective arts education enables young people to develop the wide range of their own intellectual capabilities and to make sense of the different qualities of their experience. An education which aims to develop the full range and power of young people's intellectual abilities will certainly emphasise mathematics, science and verbal reasoning. It will also give equal weight to the arts.

Aesthetic development

75. Aesthetic perception is a response to the formal qualities of objects and events. In the arts these qualities are controlled and refined to create forms of expression which embody the artist's ideas and perceptions and which engage the observer's aesthetic sensibilities. Arts education is concerned with deepening young people's sensitivities to the formal qualities — and therefore to the pleasures and meanings — of the arts and, through this process, with extending the range and depth of their aesthetic sensibilities and judgement.

The education of feeling

76. For the most part, young people's feelings and the role of feelings in intellectual, personal and social development are not taken into account in education. Feelings and emotions are forms of evaluations. The grief we may show at a death, the elation at a birth, the pleasure at success — these are all part of our perceptions of these events and express the values we attach to them. Changes in feeling derive from changes in understanding. The task of education is to encourage young people to examine their perceptions of the situation to which their feelings relate. All curriculum work may affect the pupil's view of the world and his or her life of feeling. Work in the arts has an important role in:

- giving status and a positive place to personal feelings and values;
- enabling a direct consideration of values and of the feelings to which they relate;
- giving forms to feeling.

The exploration of values

77. The arts are deeply concerned with questions of value. This is the case in two main senses: in general, with social and moral values and, in particular, with aesthetic and artistic values. We noted above that feelings are evaluations of events. Many feelings are given a social value — as vices and virtues, for example. No teacher can go far into the education of feelings, therefore, without encountering questions of social morality and of moral education. The arts offer positive and immediate ways of raising questions of value and of exploring the cultural perceptions to which they relate.

78. Arts education is also concerned with enabling young people to make informed and increasingly discriminating judgements about their own and other people's work in the arts. Artistic judgement of existing work is not simply a matter of expressing personal preferences and tastes. It requires:

- objectivity in specifying the qualities and characteristics of the work which support the judgement;
- clarification of the aesthetic and artistic values on which the judgement is based;
- an appropriate conceptual vocabulary with which to formulate and express judgements.

Physical and perceptual skills

79. Arts education involves the development of many different kinds of skill. These include the technical skills that pupils require for controlling different media of expression, the perceptual skills of observation, composition and evaluation, and the discourse skills for talking and writing about work. The arts also call on a wide range of social skills which are vital to the collaborative work needed in many arts projects. In these and other respects the arts also contribute in significant ways to personal and social education.

Personal and social education

80. Much of the curriculum is based on a specific view of academic abilities. All pupils have these abilities to one degree or another and some are especially gifted in this area. All pupils also have a wide range of other intellectual and creative abilities. The predominant concern with conventional academic work has often meant that other, equally important, capabilities have been neglected in schools. All pupils may suffer from this neglect in terms of personal achievement, and some suffer irreversibly from a sense of failure by the specific standards of success that schools have cherished (Hargreaves 1982). The arts provide all pupils with the opportunities to explore a fuller range of their abilities, and some pupils with the chance to discover for the first time where their real abilities lie. The experience of success in achievement, and enjoyment in learning which the arts demonstrably promote can raise immeasurably the self-esteem of young people and their estimation of their own abilities and, as DES (1978) has shown, greatly increase their motivation for learning across the curriculum.

The ethos of the school

81. The arts can contribute enormously to the general quality and morale of school life. A sense of community is formed through shared events such as concerts, exhibitions, plays and other performances; likewise through displays of pupils' work throughout the school, and the respect for the pupils' achievements that this demonstrates. The arts also contribute significantly to the ethos of the school, both from within the daily curriculum, and from the increased motivation that comes from all pupils having a rich and varied education with opportunities to experience success on many fronts.

SUMMARY

82. In this chapter we have related our definition of the arts to the aims of the whole curriculum and argued that they are an essential element of cultural education. We related this idea to multicultural education and argued that arts education must extend beyond the styles and conventions of Western/European culture. Against this background we identified a number of more specific roles of the arts in schools. We will develop these points in Chapter Five, where we look at the main elements and modes of arts practice in education. In Chapter Four we discuss the way in which the main principles to have emerged from the discussion in this chapter might influence the range of arts provision in the curriculum as a whole.

THE ARTS IN THE CURRICULUM

INTRODUCTION

83. What range of provision is needed for the arts in the curriculum? The National Curriculum identifies art and music as foundation subjects; drama is included within English, and dance as part of physical education. On the basis of our general analysis of the arts and arts education, this chapter identifies a minimum arts entitlement for all pupils. It argues that the arts should be provided for within a common policy, and we identify the principles on which this provision might be based. We look at the relationships between the arts in the curriculum, and at the distinctions between them. On this basis we discuss the relationships between the arts and other areas of the curriculum including media education, design and technology and crafts education. We begin by distinguishing two main roles of the arts in schools.

LEARNING IN AND THROUGH THE ARTS

84. In describing the roles of the arts in the curriculum, a distinction can be made between learning *in* and learning *through* the arts. Although deriving from innate capacities, mature achievement and understanding in any of the arts call for increasingly sophisticated skills and knowledge. The distinctive roles of arts education are to deepen young people's knowledge of and competence in the arts:

- to develop the concepts and skills which will enable young people to use the processes of the arts;
- to widen their knowledge and understanding of the arts;
- to develop their critical sensibilities.

The working processes of the arts have many applications within teaching and learning in all parts of the curriculum. They bring to life themes, issues and events in history, in social studies, science and personal and social education, and in the teaching of humanities. In learning *through* the arts, the prime focus is likely to be on the theme or subject matter, or on personal and social education; in learning *in* the arts, on the aesthetic and technical qualities of the work. These are complementary roles — in principle, at least. In practice, successful use of the arts in other areas of the curriculum depends on the teachers' and pupils' levels of expertise in the arts: learning *through* requires learning *in* the arts. This balance is not always struck in schools.

THE NEED FOR BALANCE

85. The educational experience of young people in the arts varies widely in breadth and in depth according to the attitudes of parents, staff and governors to the arts, and the school's history and traditions. Provision in many schools is unbalanced in various ways. In the topic-based curriculum of the primary school, teachers tend to emphasise the values of learning through the arts and spend too little time on learning in them. As a result they can miss opportunities to develop positive attitudes and necessary skills in the arts, leading to underachievement both in the arts and in the topics they are used to explore. Secondary schools tend to emphasise learning in the arts and can miss equally important opportunities to use the arts to enrich the curriculum as a whole. In most primary schools 'art and craft' are taught, as is some form of practical music-making. An increasing number of classroom teachers make some use of drama, but as with dance this is rarely taught in a systematic way. In some secondary schools there are vigorous and wide-ranging programmes of work; in some there is exciting work in only one or two disciplines, usually because of a particularly good department or teacher.

86. The experience of the project suggests three general principles of provision to ensure that the arts make a full contribution to young people's education. These relate to balance:

- within the curriculum as a whole;
- between the arts disciplines;
- within the teaching of the arts themselves.

Balance in the whole curriculum

87. The first principle of provision is that *all pupils should have a broad and balanced education in the arts comparable to that in other major areas of the curriculum including sciences and humanities.* The various arts disciplines have common characteristics and related roles in education. It follows that they should be planned for collectively, like sciences and humanities, as a generic area of the whole curriculum. A common policy is needed to ensure that pupils' opportunities in the arts are in balance with their educational experience as a whole and that the arts collectively have the necessary time, status and resources in relation to other major areas of the curriculum. This balance is difficult to achieve where the arts are provided for as an unrelated assortment of separate subjects. This is not to say that all of the arts are the same. Indeed one of the purposes of co-ordinated planning is to recognise differences between the arts and to relate them to pupils' individual interests and aptitudes.

Balance between the arts

88. The second principle is that *provision should be balanced between the arts.* There are two related points here: first, equal provision should be made for each of the major modes of artistic activity; second, pupils should have opportunities to specialise in areas of the arts that best suit their different aptitudes and abilities. Arts education is conventionally taken to include music, dance, drama, visual and verbal arts. In Chapter Two we discussed the cultural difficulties of defining the arts in these terms and suggested that a different classification is needed for the planning of the arts in the curriculum. We identified five elemental modes of understanding that underpin the many different cultural forms of the arts: the visual, aural, kinaesthetic, verbal and enactive modes. Young people should have experience in each of these. Artistic expression in these different modes uses a variety of media and it is these media that distinguish the conventional arts disciplines in schools. The different modes of understanding and media used in different arts disciplines offer young people very different opportunities for creative achievement and for critical understanding.

89. The performing arts make central use of time as a medium of expression. Dance uses the media of bodily movement, space and time; drama uses language, movement, space and time; music, sound and time. These forms of artistic expression exist only in performance — as they happen — and use the measures and rhythms of time for aesthetic and artistic purposes. When the performance is over the music or the dance is finished. To experience it again the performance has to be repeated. A second common characteristic of the performing arts is that they often rely on two related roles: that of the '*author*' — the composer, writer or choreographer — who conceives the work and that of the *performers* — the dancers, actors, musicians — who bring it to life. The creative relationship of performers to authors is of particular interest in educational terms and we will come back to it in the next chapter.

90. In the visual arts, the artist often creates an object which takes on an independent existence. Although it exists in time, a painting does not take place over time in the same way as a performance. It is available at once in its entirety. The observer may focus separately on its different aspects, but they are all available simultaneously. In the visual arts there is usually no performer who intervenes creatively between the artist and the observer. In the verbal arts the words are also available directly as they were written. However, the perception of the words on the page is not the artistic experience of literature. The words are the catalyst for the imaginative experiences they evoke in the reader's mind that are the essence of literary experience. The verbal mode is different in kind from the visual, and so too is the nature of the ideas and perceptions which can be expressed.

91. The distinctions between performing, visual and verbal arts are not discrete. Drama draws deeply on the verbal arts and plays are often read as literature when not seen as performances. Radio drama is closer, in some respects, to the experience of reading than of theatre. In many cultures poetry is a performing art and merges with the visual arts, drama and dance. Contemporary 'performance art' blends elements of the visual arts with those of theatre and often film. Chinese opera, as European opera, combines elements of the visual, verbal and performing arts in a single integrated discipline. So too do film and video. The relationship between the audience and a film is different from that in the theatre, where for example, the audience sees the whole stage and is free to focus on different aspects of it. In film and video the audience's attention is focused by the editing of images, backgrounds and visual textures which combines some of the time dynamics of performing arts with the visual dynamics of photography.

92. Young people do not have a general artistic ability which can be developed equally well by work in any medium. Someone who is able to think and communicate aurally will not necessarily be able to do so visually or verbally. Provision for the arts in schools should identify and respond to these differences. It follows, in general terms, that at the beginning of arts education in the primary school children should have opportunities to work in each of the five main modes of the arts — visual, aural, verbal, kinaesthetic, enactive — to discover what each offers them, and to explore where their own aptitudes and abilities lie. This is an essential foundation for later, more specialist achievements. In due course in the secondary school pupils should be allowed to concentrate on those areas of the arts that they find the most rewarding and fulfilling. Real achievement comes from close application. A curriculum which offers only one or two disciplines would be inadequate. Equally, one which required all pupils to work in all of the arts every week would be unrealistic and probably counterproductive, allowing neither the time nor the opportunities for the sustained work on which progress and attainment in the arts depends.

Balance within the arts

93. The third principle of balanced provision is that *there should be balance in the teaching of the arts between pupils' own creative work and their critical understanding of the work of other people*. At various times, as we explored in Chapter One, the balance between these has tilted one way or another, varying both historically and between the various disciplines. Not only are both of these aspects equally important in themselves, they can also be mutually enriching. This area of balance has particular implications for planning courses and for pupil assessment. We will return to it as the principal theme of the next chapter.

PROVISION IN PRIMARY SCHOOLS

94. Summarising the various points discussed above, the aims of arts provision in primary schools are to:

- stimulate interest in and awareness of the expressive and creative potential of the arts;
- introduce pupils to a wide range of media and forms of artistic expression;
- begin to develop their practical and perceptual skills in these media and forms;
- introduce them to a wide range of other people's work from a variety of cultural contexts;
- begin to develop their critical understanding and judgement of other people's work.

Work in the primary school should include regular experience in each of the main modes of the arts — visual, aural, kinaesthetic, verbal and enactive. In addition to using the arts in the teaching of themes and other subjects (learning *through* the arts), time should be allowed to focus on the development of the particular skills and concepts which are characteristic of the arts themselves (learning *in* the arts). By the end of Key Stage 2 teachers should be able to form a judgement about the individual aptitudes and interests of pupils within the various arts disciplines as a basis for further work, and some specialisation, in the secondary school.

PROVISION IN SECONDARY SCHOOLS

95. In addition to the aims of arts education in the primary school, secondary school provision should aim to:

- extend pupils' practical and perceptual skills in selected areas of the arts;
- extend and deepen their knowledge and understanding of other people's work, and of its cultural contexts;
- deepen and challenge their critical understanding and judgement of other people's work.

It is not practical for all pupils to work in all of the arts throughout their time at secondary schools. The resources do not exist and the time is not available to allow work of any depth on such a basis. Nor is it necessary. Pupils reach a point, probably in most cases by the end of Key Stage 3, when it is appropriate to concentrate on areas where their interests are sharpest. It is important to recognise that the time available for the curriculum is not one week of forty periods, but eleven years of continuous experiences. By the end of Key Stage 3 at the latest, pupils should have opportunities to specialise in one or two arts disciplines and to work in these disciplines 'on a worthwhile scale' as *Better Schools* (DES 1985a) puts it. This specialist work should be complemented by work in combined arts courses.

COMBINED ARTS

96. There has been a trend in recent years, in secondary schools in particular, towards various forms of collaborative work between arts teachers. A range of terms is used to describe these initiatives, including 'mixed media', 'integrated', 'combined', 'multidisciplinary' and 'interdisciplinary' arts. These terms are often used interchangeably; often they are all taken as synonyms for 'integrated arts'. We have found it more useful to take *combined arts* as the general term for any combination of media or modes of work and to use the term 'integration' in a more specific way. Other terms can be defined in the following ways.

- *Mixed media*
  Most combined arts work uses more than one medium. For example in the visual arts using photographs, paint and textiles to create a collage, or, in the performing arts, a piece of work involving light, sound and movement. Some combined arts work goes further and involves changes in the organisation of work in schools.
- *Multidisciplinary*
  Teachers from different disciplines, which may include maths, history and other non-arts as well as arts disciplines, may work together on an agreed theme or issue while retaining the practices and conventions of their own disciplines. For example, a music and a drama teacher may each teach their own subjects as usual but agree to work on common themes with the same groups of pupils.
- *Interdisciplinary*
  Some combined arts work involves close interaction between disciplines. Sometimes it takes the form of work overlapping — for example, an art department helping a geography course on the local

environment by teaching pupils drawing and observational skills. In other cases, it might involve a higher degree of negotiation over the nature of the work and this may affect both the form and the methods. Attempts to link a piece of writing to a piece of music, for example, may lead to adjustments in the form and understanding of both.

• *Integration*
Literally 'making whole', integration implies a more fundamental change in approaches to teaching and learning. It suggests that while separate disciplines may be identified at the outset, the process of working together involves a transformation into new forms which renders the original elements indistinguishable. From a European perspective, many non-European arts practices are integrated in this sense. Integrated arts teaching suggests the fusing of different disciplines to create new methods of work and different forms of expression.

97. In terms of our general argument, collaborative work between traditional arts specialisms in schools has much to commend it when there is a genuine partnership and sharing of expertise. We have reported on various examples of such schemes in *The Arts 5-16: Practice and Innovation*. Ironically, collaboration can sometimes work against the improvement of the arts in schools, by overturning one or more of the basic principles of provision. In some schools combined arts courses have led to a net reduction in the time and resources that were previously available to the separate specialist courses. This affects the balance of arts provision in relation to other curriculum areas. Such reductions can limit the opportunities for in-depth work, in any of the arts disciplines and affect standards of achievement. There are sound reasons for teaching the arts together at some times; the essential task in planning is to ensure that the three principles of balance enumerated here are constantly balanced with each other.

THE ARTS AND THE WHOLE CURRICULUM

98. We have outlined three principles on which balanced provision for the arts should be based. This provision should be developed as an integral part of the school's policy for the whole curriculum. As such it should also recognise the potential relationships between the arts and other areas of the curriculum. These include areas of obvious affinity, such as media education, design and technology, and crafts education, but also other curriculum areas and cross-curricular themes to which the arts can contribute in vivid and enriching ways.

Media education   **99.** In discussing definitions of the arts in Chapter Two we commented on the significance of technological developments for the practice of the arts, and for access to them. This suggests important common ground between the arts and media education. A general distinction is usually made between media education and media studies. Media *education* may be promoted by all teachers and aims to increase children's critical understanding of the media — television, film, video, radio, photography, popular music, printed materials and computer software: 'How they work, how they produce, meanings, how they are organised and how audiences make sense of them are the issues that media education addresses' (British Film Institute 1989).

Media education aims 'to create more active and critical media users who will demand and could contribute to a greater range and diversity of media products' (ibid.). Media *studies* is a term generally used to describe specialist media courses, with their own bodies of knowledge, in the upper secondary school and in further and higher education, 'or as specific modules or components within other subject areas or vocational training' (ibid.).

100. In the 1970s media studies was largely theoretical, often with a strong sociological and political content, and little or no practical media experience. The new technologies in schools (video portapacks etc.) have encouraged more classroom teachers to become involved in media education. One factor in the change of attitudes was the publication by HMI in 1983 of *Popular Television and Schoolchildren* (DES 1983). Since then the emphasis in schools has been on encouraging pupils to understand the ways in which television, cinema, newspapers, advertising etc. present particular views of the world and how they, as consumers, create meanings from them. The exploration of popular television and advertising leads directly into a study of social and institutional issues. The focus is not only on the formal features of the work itself but on the context in which it is produced and the purposes behind it.

101. Some of the central interests of arts education and media education have now begun to merge. In some respects the distinction between arts and media education is misleading. The idea of the arts as cultural education is one which is also rooted in some of the defining interests of media education. It is important therefore for teachers in these two areas to work together where possible and to exchange expertise. Arts teachers have much to bring to this relationship with their particular experiences in stimulating and sustaining practical creative work by pupils. Media educators have complementary experience in methods of critical study, particularly with regard to the economic and institutional factors involved in the promotion of some art forms and some works over others, and in issues such as the representation of race and gender. Significantly, many media teachers have been drawn from the arts and the humanities.

102. An increasing number of schools are beginning to develop work in video, computer graphics, sound recording, synthesisers etc., but the numbers are still small and few of them relate creative work in these media to a critical study of their use in popular and commercial culture. Too often video production in schools is an imitation of popular television and cinema forms without any study of the issues these forms raise about the presentation and 'framing' of material. By bringing together the most powerful contributions of arts and media education, it is possible to enable pupils to be aware, through practical analysis and through their own creative work, of the contexts in which such work is produced and understood.

Design and technology

103. Design and technology involve a number of related processes which are grouped together as a single discipline in the National Curriculum. These processes range from identifying needs and opportunities for design and technological activities, to making and appraising artefacts, systems or environments (DES 1989a). The processes of design and technology overlap in many respects with those of the arts and especially, though by no means exclusively, with the visual arts. The Parkes committee (DES 1989a, para. 1.22) emphasised in particular the area of aesthetic judgement. In design and technology,

> the fluency of pupils in the design 'language' of form, pattern, colour, texture, shape and spatial relationships is of crucial importance. Their command of this 'language' and judgement of how to apply such considerations could clearly be developed further in art.

One of the central processes of design is the 'visualisation of the artefacts, systems, environments or events that are to be created and their aptness to the practical problems they are intended to overcome' (ibid.). This involves the general processes of creative thought and intuitive judgement which are in play in the arts. The practice of design draws heavily on some of the practical and perceptual skills associated with the arts, in particular those of drawing and visual observation. It is no coincidence that *art and design* is an established term for the visual arts in schools, and that many professional designers have a visual arts background and training including frequently one in fine art.

104. Practical work in the arts involves design *and* very often technology too. The processes of making, which we discuss in the next chapter, are precisely those of developing forms which express and communicate the perceptions and ideas with which the artist is concerned. Much of the creative work of making is the testing of one approach against another in the realisation of an appropriate form. Two- and three-dimensional work in the visual arts involves a wide variety of materials and involves increasing knowledge and practical skill to select and use them. Music, drama and dance also draw on technological understanding, in the construction and use of instruments for example, and in many aspects of production and performance.

105. Tastes in design — the aesthetic criteria applied — are often forged, and certainly influenced, by developments in aesthetic style and judgement in the arts and other areas of culture. Fine art 'whether it takes the form of a painting, a vessel, a tapestry or a sculpture, influences and inspires design and manufacture and taste. Remove aesthetic experimentation and you lose good design' (O'Grady 1989). This is a telling example of the interaction of cultural processes. The essential distinction between the arts and design and technology, however, is that where the processes of design are directed to the resolution of a practical need or problem, those in the arts are directed at issues of understanding. Whereas aesthetic judgements in design relate to function, in the arts they relate to meaning.

Crafts education

106. If art is commonly linked to design in the secondary school, in the primary school it is often associated with crafts. Before the advent of the National Curriculum, crafts in the secondary school had been increasingly related to design and technology (CDT). Although crafts are sometimes still thought of in terms of hobbies and cottage industries, there was an upsurge during the 1970s and 1980s in sophisticated crafts work in ceramics, weaving, pottery, woodwork, metalwork and so on. The focus of crafts is the creation of practical and decorative objects. This includes 'things we wear and use, fashion accessories, clothes, knitwear, jewellery, utensils, furniture, wall hangings, books' (Crafts Council 1987) and so on. There has been a tendency in schools to think of crafts as the practical skills which are used in the service of other work, rather than as areas of creative and cultural achievement in their own right. It is now increasingly recognised that crafts involve a range of knowledge and achievements in themselves, including:

- knowledge and understanding of materials — and their behaviour in different states and settings;
- understanding tools and equipment — from the simplest (the hands themselves, needles, pencils, chisels) to the more complex (the lathe, wheel, loom, computer);
- manipulative skills — in working with materials, tools and equipment;
- critical judgement — in practical, technical and aesthetic issues;
- design — research and development of appropriate forms.

(ibid.)

As with design in general, there is considerable overlap between crafts processes and those of the arts, both in terms of practical skills and aesthetic judgements. The distinction between the two areas is also the same.

CROSS-CURRICULAR ISSUES

107. There are two main ways in which the arts relate to other areas of the curriculum, including the cross-curricular themes to be promoted through the National Curriculum — economic awareness, health education, personal and social education:

(a) as methods of teaching and learning; as we noted above, the techniques and processes of the arts can be used to explore, illustrate and bring to life themes and issues in a wide variety of other disciplines.

(b) as the focus of learning in other disciplines.

These opportunities for learning through the arts are developed in detail in *The Arts 5-16: Practice and Innovation.* We emphasise there the need for co-ordinating provision for the arts within a whole-curriculum policy, and for facilitating an exchange of ideas and expertise between staff, not only within the arts, but across the whole curriculum.

SUMMARY

108. In this chapter we have identified three main principles on which provision for the arts in the curriculum should be based. These were used to identify the main aims of arts education in primary and secondary schools and to consider the relationship between specialist teaching and developments in combined arts. Finally we considered the relationships between the arts and other areas of the curriculum, in particular media education, design and technology and craft education. Early in the chapter we outlined three necessary areas of balance in arts education. The third of these concerns the balance of work within the teaching of the arts themselves. This underpins the framework for teaching and learning to which we turn in the next chapter.

Chapter five

A FRAMEWORK FOR TEACHING AND LEARNING

INTRODUCTION

109. The arts embrace a very wide range of media, activities and roles, from composing poetry to playing in orchestras and bands, from making prints and performing in plays to watching films and visiting galleries. Recognising this variety, what range of experiences should be included in a planned arts education, and on what basis? In this chapter we identify some of the fundamental ingredients of teaching and learning in all of the arts and propose a common framework of ideas and terminology as a guide for teaching and assessment.

ACTIVITIES AND PROCESSES

110. From some points of view the relationships between the arts can be difficult to see. Certainly this is true if comparisons are made between the many *activities* of the various arts disciplines. Putting paint on canvas is obviously different from dancing or playing the flute, and the practical skills involved and the sorts of works which result are different too. Most of what is written and said about arts teaching is specific to individual disciplines. There are many books available, for example, which give teachers helpful advice on specific things to do and resources to use. As useful as such books are, they can also help to disguise the similarities which exist between disciplines, not at the level of activities, which are plainly different, but in terms of the underlying processes, which are fundamentally the same.

111. Although the pianist trying the first notes of a new composition is engaged in a different activity from the sculptor making the first marks on a piece of clay, they are engaged in similar processes of exploration which are common to art-making in all media. It is these underlying processes which substantiate the place of the arts in education and which teachers, in planning the specific activities of arts lessons, should promote. Although a curriculum plan will include details of activities, it should be based on a conception of what these activities are for. The framework we offer here begins by identifying two dimensions of arts education:

(a) two ways of engaging in the arts;

(b) four elements of learning.

TWO WAYS OF ENGAGING IN THE ARTS

112. There are two general ways of engaging in the arts. Individuals can be involved in producing their own original work and they can be involved in responding to existing work. We refer to these respectively as *making* and *appraising*. We noted in Chapter Three that in the practice of the arts young people can be enabled to clarify and communicate their own ideas and values: that through critical engagement with existing work they can be brought into vivid contact with the ideas, values and sensibilities of other people in their own and in other cultural communities. Making and appraising are equally important and mutually enriching aspects of cultural education. What are the characteristics of making and appraising, and how are they related?

Making

113. Making describes all the processes in which pupils are actively producing their own work. Making may be an individual or a group process. It includes work originated by the individual or group and the performance of other people's material, including scores and scripts. Making is literally what artists do, creating physical objects — paintings, sculptures, prints and so on, and events — music, a dance, a drama. Making in the arts is both a conceptual and a practical process. It is conceptual in the sense that it is concerned with ideas and understanding. It is practical in that artists explore ideas through the manipulation of various media — sounds, words, images, movement, paint, clay and so on — to create forms which embody their perceptions. Making is not only a way of expressing ideas, but a way of having ideas. Just as a grasp of mathematics can lead to the generation of ideas which are otherwise inconceivable, so the ability to make music or to dance or paint opens up forms of aural, kinaesthetic and visual thinking which are otherwise inaccessible. Arts education should enable young people to get inside these ways of thinking and to generate new insights for themselves.

Appraising

114. Appraising describes all the processes through which young people engage with existing work. This includes reflecting critically on their own work as well as on other people's work. We use the term appraising to suggest the need for critical judgement and discrimination. Individual response to specific works includes their direct sensory appeal — with music, for example, to its immediate tonal and rhythmic qualities; with photography, painting and sculpture to their direct visual presence. Arts education should deepen young people's sensibilities to actual works by making them more aware of these qualities. A knowledge of artistic concepts and terminology is necessary to facilitate critical perception of other people's work and to articulate personal responses.

115. Artists work within particular cultural settings and with particular and diverse intentions. Understanding their work requires some knowledge of the context and conventions within which it was made, and of its purposes. One role of arts education is to deepen young people's understanding of the diversity and purposes of the arts in different cultural settings. They should be enabled to understand the different ways in which the arts are produced and used socially and economically, and to develop a critical understanding not just of individual works, but of the arts as cultural processes, institutions and, often, commodities.

THE PROCESSES OF THE ARTS

116. Making and appraising involve a number of related processes, and it is these that the activities of arts education should promote. These processes include exploring, forming, performing, presenting, responding and evaluating.

Exploring   **117.** The arts are ways of exploring and investigating ideas. In improvised drama for example, a group looking at the social issues of poverty may experiment with a variety of situations and roles to explore their different perceptions, to formulate and share ideas around the theme. Equally, individuals or groups may use the forms and media of visual arts, dance, music or writing in the same speculative ways to open up areas of interest and to begin to shape their ideas about them. This exploratory work need not lead to a finished piece for others to see; it may be tentative and its outcomes immediate and self-fulfilling. Exploratory work is also important in the media of the arts in developing new forms and techniques of expression, experimenting with new materials, movements, colours and sounds to test their range and potential.

Forming   **118.** Making involves the forming of objects or events which embody the artists' ideas and perceptions. These perceptions are not simply translated into dramatic, visual or musical forms. They are conceived as dramatic, visual or musical ideas whose meanings are only fully available in that form. Change the form and the meaning is changed. The initial idea for a new work may be vague and unfocused and the first form only very approximate: some jotted notes, a sketch, a tentative phrase of movements, a first model or maquette. The process of making is one of working on the form itself and of bringing ideas into clearer focus. Ideas are often reassessed, reworked, refined and clarified through shaping the form in what Robert Witkin (1974), echoing George Kelly (see para. 52), describes as a process of 'successive approximations'. It is only in the making that the artist discovers what the right gesture, rhythm or sound may be to make the idea intelligible through an appropriate form.

Performing   **119.** In the performing arts there are two related and dependent processes of making: that of the author — the choreographer, dramatist or composer who originates the work — and that of the performers who bring it to life. Performing is a process of re-making. Working on a role in a play, interpreting a dance or musical composition can be as creative as the original act of composition, as the performer evolves a personal interpretation of the work. A dramatic text or musical or choreographic score suggests a performance, it does not determine it. Grotowski has observed for example that:

> All the great texts represent a sort of deep gulf for us. Take Hamlet. Professors will tell us, each for himself, that they have discovered an

objective Hamlet. They suggest to us revolutionary Hamlets, rebel and impotent Hamlets, Hamlet the outsider etc. But there is no objective Hamlet. The strength of great works really consists in their catalytic effect: they open doors....

(Grotowski 1968, p.57)

Presenting

120. Presenting is any process of sharing work with another person and ranges from sharing ideas, notes and preparatory studies in the classroom to participation in public performances and exhibitions. Sometimes this may be to other members of the class, the rest of the school and sometimes more publicly through performances and exhibitions. Presenting is a natural and informal part of any arts lesson as, for example, in the discussions which take place about work in progress between pupils and with the teacher. Presenting always involves an audience, however informal. The experience of sharing work with other people, of having their responses and testing their perceptions can be positive and beneficial for all pupils. The sense of audience can also be a powerful and valuable influence in sharpening the focus of individual work and its powers of communication. Presenting requires pupils to pay careful attention to detail and to how their work is displayed or performed to best effect. Pupils should be encouraged to experiment with different ways of presenting and contextualising their own work. The appraisals of others can greatly increase their sense of ownership and pride in their work and can be a significant stimulus to further work and development.

Responding

121. The arts are concerned at all stages with personal response. They are formed out of responses to ideas, experiences and events and they exist as ways of fashioning and articulating those responses. Forming is a reciprocal process of shaping and responding to an emergent form of expression until the work captures and conveys the artist's perceptions. Understanding existing work also requires a creative response by the 'audience'. We commented in Chapter Two that judgements about the artistic status and qualities of existing work often involve different criteria and always involve personal values. An audience watching a play or a group of individuals looking at a piece of visual art may have many different interpretations and responses. This is partly because individual responses are influenced by the values and attitudes we bring to the work as much as by what the work itself presents to us. Arts education should aim to deepen and extend young people's responses to existing work by helping them to be more aware of artistic and aesthetic styles and qualities, and of the values and criteria which influence their own responses.

Evaluating

122. We distinguished in Chapter Two between artistic and aesthetic experience. Artistic judgement requires some knowledge of cultural styles, practices and conventions. Arts education should strengthen young people's abilities to make judgements about existing work by extending their knowledge about the arts: about their forms and functions in different cultures and their different histories and traditions. A key objective is to increase the objectivity of young people's judgements about their own and other people's work. Critical judgements should be objective in the sense of being supported by evidence in the work itself, and related to clear criteria. The development of appropriate language is central to pupils' understanding of their experience in the arts as in all areas of learning. Arts education should

help young people to develop a vocabulary of ideas and terminology with which to describe the characteristics of different work and to articulate their own judgements.

> In music,
>
> > An important way in which the objectivity of appraising can be demonstrated is by the identification of criteria upon which judgements should be based. In performance, for instance, sense of style, good phrasing, accuracy in pitch and rhythm and balance between parts might be sought... with appropriate exploitation of instruments and voices and with the composer's sense of texture.... No criteria should be applied in a mechanistic way. The appropriate criteria and their respective performance will differ for each composition.
> >
> > (MANA 1986, p.12)

123. The different processes of making and appraising are intimately related. A piece of work may provide the opportunity for pupils to engage in all of these aspects of the arts. Their responses to the work of other people will stimulate new work of their own; their experience of making will deepen their understanding and enrich their perceptions of existing work. There are, however, logical distinctions to be made between the various modes and processes. Pupils need to have acquired certain concepts and skills before they can begin making. Something must have been made before it can be presented, and presented before it can be appraised. At each stage the pupils need to have learnt certain ideas and information in order to proceed and they acquire new skills and information as the work progresses.

PROCESS AND PRODUCT

124. It is sometimes said that the real value of arts education is the process rather than the product. There is some truth in this. The distinction is false if it is taken to mean that the quality of the finished work is irrelevant to the process of making it, or that making itself is more important than appraising. There are two sorts of product in the arts. One is *conceptual*—changes in understanding; the other *formal*—the art object or event itself. The process of making does not always result in formal products. Changes in understanding can occur throughout the process of making, not only at its apparent conclusion in a finished or realised form. For this reason pupils' involvement in the exploratory processes of the arts is important in itself. Not all works are finished or intended to be seen by an audience.

125. The role of the teacher requires flexible and sensitive responses to pupils' interests and abilities. Teachers need to be able to judge when a pupil's particular piece of work has run its course or when it can be moved forward, and when pupils' work can be enhanced by engaging with other people's work. Through discussing work in progress, helping pupils to step back and reflect on what is emerging, and supporting them with advice and information as necessary. Pupils can be helped to make connections between their own art-making and the variety of cultural forms which surround them.

THE ELEMENTS OF LEARNING

126. We have identified making and appraising as the two main ways of engaging in the arts, and discussed some of the processes involved. Making and appraising are one dimension of our framework for planning courses. The other distinguishes four main *elements of learning* in the arts:

(a) concepts
(b) skills
(c) attitudes and values
(d) information

Concepts

127. Artistic activity involves artistic intentions. Though they may produce works with aesthetic intentions and merits, young children cannot *intentionally* produce works of art without some understanding of concepts of art. Artistic intentions require artistic conceptions. Young people develop such conceptions as they grow, just as they learn about other aspects of their cultural environment. Arts education partly consists in extending pupils' conceptual understanding of the arts. Such concepts can be broadly distinguished into two groups: contextual and aesthetic.

Contextual concepts

128. There is no universal, defining feature of art which crosses all historical or cultural boundaries. What counts as art in one time and place may not in another. Young people develop conceptions of the arts not by definition but by growing acquaintance with artistic practices and conventions; and these are bound up in the complex networks of values and ideas — religious, moral, political and so on — of different cultures. Consequently, artistic evaluations require an understanding of the context in which a work was made. Relevant concepts include *genre, period* and *convention.* In exploring such concepts in music for example, pupils should have opportunities to hear, discuss and evaluate many forms of music including orchestral, jazz, popular, non-European and music used in advertising, films and television. They should consider the formal differences between them and the audiences they attract. Concepts of context are not only important in appraising other people's work. It is just as important that children should see that their own work is growing within cultural contexts which are likely to exercise a strong influence on its form and style.

Aesthetic concepts

129. Aesthetic concepts relate to the form and organisation of the work itself. Relevant concepts include *rhythm, repetition, unity, symmetry, contrast, sequence, climax, balance, harmony, counterpoint, line, colour, texture, pace* and *tone.* Some of these are common to many disciplines, others are more specific, such as pitch and volume in music; body, shape and personal space in dance. Many aesthetic concepts are culturally specific. Malaysian theatre for example is rooted in the interpretation of traditional myths and legends. It has an episodic structure which is quite different from the European dramatic unities of time, place and situation. Where Western classical music is essentially linear and climactic in structure, Malay music is cyclical and repetitive. These aesthetic conventions reflect a deep structure of cultural values and beliefs about the cyclical nature of individual existence. The aesthetic system is rooted in a metaphysical system.

130. Cultural differences can be of considerable significance for classroom planning. Concepts such as 'harmony' or 'depiction' are more typical of some cultures than others. Some children in our culturally diverse society will not be familiar with their conventions. Arts education should enable pupils to recognise and understand the variety of concepts — contextual and aesthetic — which underpin arts practice, recognising that young people come to school with many different cultural experiences. A mutual sharing and understanding of these concepts can enrich the understanding of all children and teachers.

Skills   **131.** The arts are natural forms of expression in the sense that they grow out of innate capacities in us all. But sophisticated expression in the arts is not a result of simple maturation. The ability to play an instrument or to achieve complex visual effects in paint or movement is not an inevitable result of getting older. Creative work in the arts, as in all other areas of human achievement, needs skills and expertise which have to be learnt and practised. There are three main groups of skills which arts education should aim to develop in all pupils: *perceptual, productive* and *discursive*.

Perceptual skills

132. The arts are forms of description. Observation is a central skill in all art forms. In visual arts, observational drawing is practised not just for its own sake but to sharpen perceptions of the visual environment as a basis for all forms of visual representation. Similarly in literature, dance and drama, the observation and description of actual experience is the foundation for creative work of all sorts. Perceptual skills are essential in shaping and organising materials into appropriate forms. The artist incorporates aesthetic qualities in the work to affect the observer's perception and responses. Pupils can be made more sensitive to such qualities by the teacher's questioning and by experience of observation, description and interpretation.

Productive skills

133. Making involves skill and control in the manipulation of the chosen media. It is sometimes argued that teaching skills can impede a natural spontaneity in children which is necessary for genuine creative work. An emphasis on learning skills without proper opportunities to use them is certainly frustrating and self-defeating. So too is encouraging young people to express their ideas freely without giving them the means to do so effectively. For all pupils there are times when their creative ambition outruns their ability. They cannot formulate their ideas in the arts because the media they need to use are beyond their control. Teaching skills in the media is essential as part of the development of creative work.

134. The dancer is not impeded by skill in movement, nor the writer by a grasp of grammar and syntax. It is important that technical skills are developed alongside and through creative work. At times it is necessary to concentrate on skills. In dance pupils will sometimes need to reproduce as accurately as possible movements prescribed and demonstrated by the teacher. Precise instruction may be needed in handling musical instruments, art materials and the equipment of technological media, such as cameras, video, audiotape, or keyboards. These skills can liberate creative energies if taught in the proper relationship to them, not as ends in themselves, but as means to ends.

Discursive skills

135. Pupils should be enabled to develop a vocabulary and understanding of the arts which can sharpen discrimination in their own work and in their responses to the work of other people. These abilities can be encouraged through pupils:

- talking to each other and the teacher, and writing about their own work;
- responding to and learning about the work of other artists;
- visiting galleries, museums, theatres and concerts;
- meeting and working with artists and artists in residence.

Developing pupils' critical understanding of other people's work should include encouraging them to make use of and respond to each other's work, through displays, performances and exhibitions, and to make discerning judgements based on clear criteria.

Values and attitudes

136. We argued in Chapter Three that the arts are deeply concerned with questions of value and that this is so in two main senses: in general with personal, social and moral values; and in particular with aesthetic and artistic values. As the Gulbenkian report (1982) observes, an education that sets out to help young people to make sense of and contribute to the world in which they live must be concerned with helping them to investigate their own and other people's values. Artists are characteristically concerned with such things, with the evaluation and revaluation of the world around them. Working in the arts engages young people directly in expressing their own values and perceptions and in responding to the values of others.

137. Successful work in the arts requires positive attitudes to them and an interest in the forms of understanding and processes of work that they promote. Attitudes that should be encouraged through arts education include:

- the confidence to make independent judgements;
- the willingness to consider different social and artistic values, beyond the pupils' direct experience;
- the readiness to search for alternative solutions to problems;
- an openness to the work of others;
- a curiosity about the arts, their cultural roles and means of production;
- sensitivity to other people's feelings and points of view;
- a sense of self-worth resulting from positive achievement.

Information

138. Whichever process pupils are involved in, in order to proceed they will need relevant information, either about the media and materials being used — including their own bodies, voices etc. — or about the historical, artistic and social context of the work they are experiencing. In discussing the elements of learning HMI (1985b) use the term 'knowledge' where we are now using 'information'. HMI's use tends to imply factual or propositional knowledge. 'Information' seems a better term for this, and thus allows 'knowledge' to include non-propositional forms. This is particularly important in a framework for the arts. Relevant information in arts teaching includes that which enhances pupils' understanding of:

- the media and how to use them, e.g. the dynamics of harmony in music, the mechanics and restrictions of the muscles and joints in dance, the properties of pigments and colours in visual art;
- the context and conventions of other people's work.

Information should have an important contribution to make to the development of the concepts, skills and attitudes. It should be 'worth knowing; comprehensible; capable of sustaining interest; useful, now and in the future' (DES 1985b).

A FRAMEWORK FOR DEVELOPMENT

139. The figure below shows the general relationships between making and appraising and the four elements of learning in the arts. It can be filled in with the further details we have described: the types of skill and concept, the different processes of making and appraising and so on. We have not included all of these details here for fear of losing the basic purpose of the diagram, that of offering a simple guide to our proposed framework. There is, however, a point beyond which generalisations cannot be made; where the special characteristics of different disciplines need to be identified. The productive skills needed in music are different from those of fine art or dance. Within music the skills needed for keyboard playing are different from those needed for wind or untuned instruments. The specific concepts and critical terminology of dance are different from those of literature and drama, and they differ within the specialist traditions of dance.

ELEMENTS OF LEARNING	WAYS OF ENGAGING	
	Making	*Appraising*
Concepts		
Skills		
Values/Attitudes		
Information		

140. The purpose of the framework outlined here is to provide a basis for analysing teaching and learning, and for evaluating its range and quality. This project's practical work in schools confirmed that there are many examples of excellent work drawing on the wide resources of the arts. Looking generally at arts education, however, there has been an uneven history of provision across the age range and disciplines. Some teachers have made only limited use of the arts, focusing, for example, on the exploratory aspects of making, and not acknowledging the significance of developing practical skills in the media, or the fertile relationships between making and appraising. Others have focused on the factual aspects of appraising, paying too little attention to developing critical judgement and sensibility.

141. We found relatively few examples of arts teaching in which cross-cultural or cross-disciplinary studies are made and fewer still which look at questions of genre, style, production and so on as ways of organising material. Historically, the balance of work in terms of modes and elements of the arts has varied considerably in the different disciplines. For some time the teaching of skills was questioned because they were thought to impede the spontaneity of expression which was believed to be necessary for genuine creative experience. In the same way, appraising was questioned because it seemed less important than – even irrelevant to – getting children to express their own ideas. Our contention is that these different emphases revealed partial conceptions of the potential of the arts in schools. In a properly balanced arts education each of these areas of the arts has an important and dynamic relationship with the others.

SUMMARY

142. In this chapter we have offered a planning guide for teaching and assessment. This identifies making and appraising as two main ways of engaging in the arts, plus a number of processes common to all arts disciplines. We described four main elements of learning which form the second dimension of the framework and argued that a balanced arts education will give equal weight to all of these. In the next chapter we use this framework to discuss the assessment of pupils' progress and attainment in the arts.

Chapter six

ASSESSING PROGRESS

INTRODUCTION

143. Describing and judging pupils' progress in the arts are difficult and often controversial matters. There are fundamental difficulties in saying what progress is. Teachers have been further concerned that some of the traditional approaches to assessment in schools have been inimical to the arts. The Gulbenkian report (1982) particularly criticised the practice of norm-referencing — of comparing pupils' attainments against each other in reaching relative grades — and argued for assessment methods based on individual performance against agreed criteria for all pupils. The report of the Government's Task Group on Assessment and Testing (DES 1987) came to similar conclusions for all subjects. The assessment schemes of the National Curriculum are criterion-referenced, and this has created a new and, we think, positive climate for tackling assessment in the arts. In this chapter we identify some of the particular difficulties of describing and assessing progress in the arts and describe an approach to dealing with them based on the general framework for planning which we presented in the last chapter.

DIFFICULTIES IN ASSESSMENT

144. Teachers have encountered two main difficulties in tackling issues of pupils assessment in the arts: the first in describing what progress actually is, and in specifying appropriate attainment targets; the second in reconciling the principles of arts education with some of the apparently contradictory expectations of conventional assessment.

Models of progress   **145.** Progress in education is often assumed to follow a linear sequence of development from one stage to the next. Having learnt certain ideas or mastered particular skills, the pupils is assumed to move on to those which logically follow. Some researchers have attempted to identify what the sequential stages of development in the arts might be. Perhaps because they provide objects to study which are not so available in other arts subjects, most of this work has been done in the visual arts. The objects studied have tended to be produced within particular cultural styles and traditions, usually those of Western/European art. This raises doubts about claims to have identified 'natural' stages of development in children's art. Several studies comment, for example, that at about the same age children develop a sense of perspective in their drawing. This may be so in cultures where perspective is an accepted convention in visual art. In others where it is not, this 'natural' achievement does not take place.

146. Even when evidence for 'universal' theories of development has been found in the art of children of different cultures, these cultures have usually experienced a strong European influence. In other studies, European conventions and expectations have informed the research assumptions and methods of enquiry. These qualifications do not invalidate the research. But they do illustrate further the importance of the cultural assumptions and context in which ideas and perceptions are developed. Teaching can and should draw upon available theories of development. This is not to say that there is only one natural or correct model of development.

147. The difficulty is not only in saying what the stages of age-related development might be. The arts cover a very wide range of experiences, processes and activities, from the acquisition of practical skills and the learning of information to the expression of personal values, thought and feelings. There is a logical sequence to the learning of some practical skills in the arts: at some ages children are incapable of certain skills because of physical immaturity. Equally, some concepts are beyond the grasp of children of certain ages, in the arts as in all disciplines. But creative achievement and critical understanding in the arts are also affected by other factors: by cultural background, motivation, personal insight and depth of feeling. These are not stereotyped by age. A child of eight may be capable of insights and qualities of work which are beyond the reach of an adolescent or adult. In all cases there is a personal dimension to work in the arts which assessment should include.

Styles of assessment

148. The second area of difficulty in assessment is that some methods and criteria are inappropriate in the arts. At one level, some teachers worry that the act of assessment can introduce elements of judgement and criticism which can inhibit the creative relationship which is needed with pupils. We may have said enough in earlier chapters about the necessity for critical judgement in the arts to offset the main part of this concern. More generally teachers are concerned that the tendency in some forms of assessment to reduce achievement to grades or percentages concentrates attention on those aspects of the arts which lend themselves most readily to these techniques. The effect is to distort the curriculum to fit the demands of assessment. A third concern in this regard is that assessment implies objective judgement and, it is sometimes argued, the arts are primarily about subjective experience. We return to this argument below.

149. Despite these various concerns it is clear that assessment in the arts is possible and that it is necessary. Effective teachers of the arts are assessing pupils' work all of the time, otherwise they would be in no position to help them move forward. The task is to make the processes of assessment explicit and coherent. The qualitative and criterion-referred assessment schemes of the National Curriculum have emerged from a more general recognition of such difficulties in all subjects.

THE ROLES OF ASSESSMENT

150. A coherent process of assessment will fulfil four essential roles in arts education. It will:

(a) facilitate individual progress and attainment;
(b) facilitate curriculum continuity;
(c) improve co-ordination between disciplines;
(d) meet the needs of accountability.

Progress and attainment

151. Children do not become skilful and knowledgeable in the arts simply by getting older. The arts are sophisticated forms of thinking and communication which operate through complex forms of symbolic representation. Facilitating these developments is what arts education is for. Teachers need constantly to make judgements about pupils' work in order to identify existing levels of development and to plan future work. Assessment in this sense should be *formative*. Teachers also need to make overall assessments of pupils' achievements at the end of a course or period of work. Assessment should also, therefore, be *summative*.

Curriculum continuity

152. Easing the transitions between the primary and secondary phases of education, and between secondary and further and higher education, was a major area of concern within the Arts in Schools project. To achieve an easing of transition there are two requirements. The first is an agreed framework for development which extends across the whole period of compulsory education and which makes clear the relationships between general education in the arts during this period and the specialist programmes of tertiary education. Without a common and shared set of expectations, teachers in different phases of education are in no position to build on or anticipate each other's work with the same pupils. The second requirement is for an effective system of conveying information about the attainments and experiences of individual pupils as they move on. This is a principal role of assessment.

Co-ordination between disciplines

153. The arts promote developments which may influence work in other areas of the curriculum. For example, skills of drawing and observation may feed in to work in science and mathematics; the verbal and social skills developed in drama may feed in to all areas of the curriculum. Conversely, what is learnt in other subjects may affect performance and attainment in the arts. A policy for assessment in the arts should be an integral part of an assessment policy for the school as a whole, to enable arts teachers to relate their work with pupils to work in other subjects, and other teachers to take similar account of work in the arts.

Accountability

154. Many groups and individuals have a right to information about pupils' progress and attainment in school, including their work in the arts. These include the pupils themselves, their parents, other teachers, future employers and, where relevant, institutions of further and higher education.

PRINCIPLES OF ASSESSMENT

155. With these considerations in mind, a policy and process of assessment in the arts should fulfil four principles:

(a) coherence
(b) differentiation
(c) compatibility
(d) objectivity

Coherence

156. For the most part, assessment policies in the different arts disciplines have been drawn up separately. One illustration of this is the development of the GCSE national criteria for music and for art and design. Separate operations resulted in apparently inconsistent approaches to assessment between two related areas of the curriculum. Art and design identified three domains: the *conceptual, productive* and *contextual and critical.* Music also identified three domains: *experience, skills* and *communication/response.* There is a good deal of overlap in the thinking behind these different approaches. The differences in presentation may be due to lack of dialogue across the disciplines in their formulation. There are difficulties for schools in trying to develop practical and coherent approaches to assessment in the arts if they seem to need a new policy for every discipline. A unified framework makes possible more coherent practice, and helps in itself to fulfil the roles of assessment in increasing co-ordination between disciplines. This is not to say that the disciplines should be assessed as if they were identical in all respects.

Differentiation

157. Development in the arts is multifaceted. Some attainments, such as practical skills and grasp of concepts are sequential and can be related to age; others are not. Assessment should recognise different types of attainment and allow for the different rates at which children of the same ages might achieve them. A school assessment policy should allow for differences between disciplines. Many practical skills of dance, for example, are different from those of drama or music.

158. In some forms of dance it is best to begin work with pupils of primary age when their muscles and joints are supple and responsive. Older children with no early experience will be limited in their potential to master certain dance techniques. To some extent this is true of playing instruments. Young children have an appetite and capability for acquiring musical concepts and skills which older children have to work much harder to obtain. In drama and verbal arts, age is not so important in learning skills. Adolescent pupils and adults can come to drama with no practical disadvantages from starting relatively late. They may have difficulties of attitude. Teachers of older pupils coming fresh to drama often encounter an obstructive embarrassment at taking the kinds of social risk on which successful drama can depend. A common framework should not blur these differences in attainment between disciplines; it should be a means of bringing them into sharper focus.

Compatibility

159. An assessment of someone's performance involves two elements: a *description* and a *comparison.* To say that someone can play a particular piece on the recorder is a neutral description of an ability and not in itself an assessment. To say that he or she plays the piece well, or even in tune, involves a comparison with an external standard or criterion of musicianship. It is in making the comparison that the description becomes an assessment. Some forms of assessment have relied heavily on unelaborated comparisons in the form of grades and percentage marks. There are several problems in applying these techniques in the arts. First, they give little or no descriptive information. To say that a pupil has a C or B or 65 per cent is only informative to those who know the full meaning of the code. Few pupils, parents or employers do. Second, they fail to record the complexity of the experiences on which the assessment is based. Third, and perhaps most importantly, they imply that whatever is important in education can be quantified in these ways. The arts, by contrast, are to do with qualities of experience and achievement and do not lend themselves in key respects to these quantitative judgements.

160. If assessment is to be formative and summative, the forms it takes must be compatible with the sophisticated experiences on which it reports. There are two implications to this. First, statements of assessment should be separated into the two distinct elements of description and comparison. They should include a descriptive account of what pupils have actually done and of the experiences they have had. Second, in offering judgements of achievement, statements of assessment should be clear about, and should state, the criteria for comparison that are being used. Is the work being compared with that of other children? With children all of the same age? With the pupil's own previous work? To some view of the pupil's potential? To professional standards? Separating description and comparison is important if statements of assessment are to reflect the complexities of achievement in the arts. Such separation also makes available to other assessors the information and criteria on which the assessments are based, and allows other uses to be made of this information — and other judgements to be formed. Finally, and in doing all of this, it increases the necessary objectivity of assessment in the arts.

Objectivity

161. 'Objective' is often wrongly taken to mean 'provable by mathematical or scientific means' (Aspin 1984, p.6). 'Subjective', by contrast, is taken as 'reducible in the final analysis to personal preference and taste' (ibid.). Taste and preference have their place in judgements about all work in the arts — including pupils' work. Intuition and personal insight are also important qualities in forming judgements, not only in the arts, but in science and other disciplines. Objectivity is not at odds with taste or intuition, nor is it confined to the procedures and standards of mathematics and science. Objective judgements in any sphere have two necessary characteristics: first, they should be based on evidence and refer to it; second, they should be made in accordance with agreed criteria. To say, in any context, that judgements are objective is not to guarantee that they are correct or incontrovertible. It is to make them available to the comments and criticisms of others using the same evidence and criteria. Judgements of pupils' work and of their educational progress and attainment in the arts need to be objective in this sense.

EVIDENCE OF ATTAINMENT

162. Assessment, whether formative or summative, requires *evidence* of attainment. In the arts the evidence is in the observable results of pupils' creative and critical work. Creative activity has public outcomes: ideas, events, objects, which others can perceive. Evidence of making is available as the work is being formed and in its final form. As work emerges it is possible to observe and assess pupils' abilities to experiment, select, respond, develop ideas etc. through the practical competences they exhibit. Evidence of appraising is available in the statements pupils make in writing or in discussion, and in creative responses to other people's work perceptible in their own work.

ACTION AND ACT OF ASSESSMENT

163. The process of assessment partly consists of gathering such evidence as a basis for informed judgements. It is useful in this respect to distinguish between the *action* and the *act* of assessment. By the action of assessment we mean the collection of material about pupils' work as it goes on so as to provide a record of relevant experiences. This not only includes examples of work, but impressions about it and the development of clear criteria against which the work can be judged, both in general and in the individual cases. By the act of assessment we mean the making of judgements in the light of the evidence which is available. This involves the considered application of criteria which are agreed to be relevant to the work in hand. Once assessments are made they need to be acted on, to influence the course of future work.

164. The action of assessment may include pupils keeping diaries about their own work, as well as the teacher's own observation. Pupils' diaries and portfolios can have several positive functions: encouraging pupils to keep an account of their own experiences at school; to be more observant about them; to reflect critically on their own work; to become more positively engaged in their own education. Acts of assessment require the specification of criteria against which the work is being judged.

CRITERIA OF ASSESSMENT

165. The assessment of progress and attainment needs to be related to agreed criteria. In detail, these criteria will depend on various factors, such as the purpose of the work, whether it is part of a general or a specialist course, and at what level. They will also relate to the extent to which teachers are concerned with learning *in* or *through* the arts. In the first case, the criteria may be entirely arts-related, and will vary in detail between the different disciplines; in the second, they will be influenced by the theme or topic which the arts are being used to explore. The specification of detailed criteria has to be made in relation to such considerations. More broadly, it is possible to identify common learning objectives for the arts which may serve as a guide in developing specific criteria, and the general principles of progression to which they are related.

AREAS FOR ASSESSMENT

166. The framework described in Chapter Five and the assumptions discussed in earlier chapters on which it is based suggest a number of areas for assessment and general learning objectives in the arts. We outline them here to illustrate the desirability and feasibility of having clear objectives in the arts, as in other areas of the curriculum. They relate to the period of compulsory education from 5 to 16 and exemplify desirable attainments at age 16. The categorisation proposed presents typical objectives for all of the arts. This provides a basis for more specific statements of attainment within different disciplines to take account of the particular concepts and skills involved.

Making

167. Practical work in the arts involves the use and manipulation of media — sounds, images, movements, words — to create forms which clarify and express the artist's ideas and perceptions. There are two main areas of assessment: creative development, and technical development.

Creative development

This area concerns the content of pupils' own work in the arts: the nature and quality of their ideas and the forms in which they express them.

- *Objective 1*
  Pupils should demonstrate the ability to use the processes of the arts to generate and explore their own ideas and perceptions.

- *Objective 2*
  Pupils should demonstrate the ability to develop and sustain their ideas and perceptions from original conception to realised form.

Technical development

This area concerns pupils' practical skills in the use and control of the arts media, and the development of techniques in applying these skills in their own work.

- *Objective 3*
  Pupils should demonstrate the ability to control the chosen media of expression with confidence and precision.

- *Objective 4*
  Pupils should demonstrate the ability to use their practical skills appropriately within the artistic intentions of their work.

Appraising

168. Arts education is concerned with extending pupils' knowledge and understanding of the arts and with deepening their sensibilities to actual works. The way pupils respond is affected by their own values and attitudes and by their understanding of the cultural context within which the work was made and the intentions of the artist. There are two areas for assessment: critical response, and contextual understanding.

Critical response

This concerns the nature of pupils' responses to, and awareness of, the qualities of existing works in the arts and their ability to describe their responses in appropriate terms.

- *Objective 5*
  Pupils should demonstrate the ability to describe significant features of their own and others' work using relevant concepts and terminology.

- *Objective 6*
  Pupils should demonstrate the ability to make informed and discerning judgements about their own and others' work and to identify their criteria.

Contextual understanding
This area concerns pupils' knowledge and understanding of different cultural practices and conventions in the arts.

- *Objective 7*
  Pupils should demonstrate relevant knowledge and understanding of different cultural practices and traditions in the arts.

169. These general objectives make it clear that in some respects assessment tasks in the arts are conventional. In the technical and contextual areas, assessment is concerned with what children can do and what they know and understand. In other respects the assessment tasks are not conventional. In the creative and critical areas we are concerned with the nature and qualities of children's own ideas and perceptions, and ultimately with questions of value. More descriptive methods of assessment are called for here. In objectives 3 and 7 progress may be linear. Dance technique, instrumental teaching and the training of the voice for singing involve the phased development of muscular co-ordination. Complex actions and skills require the mastery of simpler, elemental skills, some of which are related to physical maturity. Similarly some concepts require a grasp of other elemental ideas. In the creative and critical areas, objectives 2, 5 and 6, progress is less obviously sequential and related to age. Some children have precocious perceptions based on personal experiences or aptitudes which are qualitatively different from those of children of the same age or older.

170. These objectives cannot be pursued mechanistically. In music for example,

> many short-term progressions based only on musical skills can be formulated. For instance, children of perhaps six or seven might usefully proceed from demonstrating a feeling for pulse by moving in time to music, or clapping the pulse and learning to articulate simple rhythms in time to it. The teacher who attempts to formulate a long-term strategy based solely on progression of this kind is doomed to failure... such progressions do not take into account the children themselves; how do they actually feel about the music concerned?... Unless music is approached as a relationship involving both giving and receiving, the pupil is unlikely to make the feeling connections which give musical activity much of its meaning.
>
> (Music Advisers National Association 1986)

PRINCIPLES OF PROGRESSION

171. These various areas of attainment in the arts are closely related. Technique (objective 4) develops alongside control of the media (objective 3). Discrimination in judgement (objective 6) is enriched by knowledge and understanding of cultural practices (objective 7). The detailed criteria of attainment in each of these areas will vary between disciplines and with the purposes of particular courses. We can identify four principles of progression to which all these criteria should relate: complexity, control, depth, and independence.

Complexity

172. We raised earlier some doubts about linear models of education in the arts. Bruner's conception of a spiral curriculum is particularly apt in this regard. Commenting on science education, he observes that the basic ideas that lie at the heart of all science and mathematics.

> and the basic themes that give form to life and literature are as simple as they are powerful. To be in command of these basic ideas, to use them effectively, requires a continual deepening of one's understanding of them that comes from learning to use them in progressively more complex forms.

> (Bruner 1966)

The same is true in the arts. The very concepts and issues which are dealt with at a simple level with young children will be revisited at increasing levels of sophistication as children grow in maturity, and as their sophistication increases in the conceptual processes of the arts themselves. A spiral curriculum is one which continually 'turns back on itself at higher levels' (ibid.).

Control　173.　Young children's first activities in the arts are playful, exploratory and often show a very loose relationship between intentions and effects. The forms used are often simple and accidental. Creative and technical development consists in acquiring increasing control of the media of expression and, as a result, in the composition of appropriate forms. These two areas of control are directly related. It is through a progression from accidental effects to eventual technical facility in the media that pupils are enabled to progress from inarticulate, derivative forms of expression to original and sophisticated work of their own.

Depth　174.　Young people have different aptitudes and interests in the arts. From the early years of primary school it is important that they should have creative and critical experiences in a wide range of artistic forms and media. During Key Stages 1 and 2 most pupils will begin to show preferences and capabilities in different disciplines. During Key Stage 3 pupils will usually be able to identify areas for specialisation within the arts. Specialisation in Key Stage 4 is necessary to acquire the depth of understanding and expertise on which articulate and fulfilling work in the arts depends, and towards which all pupils should be progressing.

Independence　175.　As they begin work in the arts young pupils depend heavily on the teacher not only for practical help and instruction, but also for their conceptions of the purposes of artistic activity, and for ideas and forms for actual work. As they progress they should be increasingly capable of originating their own ideas for work, and of making and carrying out decisions about the forms it should take. Their critical understanding should take account of the views of others but they should be increasingly capable of forming their own judgements of work and of giving reasons and criteria to support them. Mature and educated development

> will involve bringing to bear and applying all the above qualities... as well as knowledge of facts and skills so as to be able to achieve some understanding of a work's many meanings... and then maybe even be able to clarify, explain and justify that understanding to others so that their perspectives may be similarly transformed.

> (Aspin 1984)

176.　These principles of progression are of central importance in raising expectations of attainment in the arts. Too often pupils' work in the arts in schools is well beneath their practical and conceptual capabilities. Primary pupils in Year 5 or 6 for example are often given unexacting tasks in the arts of which they were capable in Years 2 or 3. However, they may not have progressed appreciably in skills or understanding during these years, either through low expectations or a lack of clear objectives. One reason is that the arts are still sometimes seen as general expressive activities which have a value in balancing the more taxing, instruction-based work of other areas of the curriculum. In this view, the very idea of learning objectives would seem out of place. The framework we have offered here is at odds with this view. The arts are exacting forms of thinking and expression, which only confer genuine rewards on young people after they have understood and gained some control over the disciplines involved.

SUMMARY

177. In this chapter we have identified some of the difficulties in describing and assessing progress and attainment in the arts. We have described four necessary roles of assessment and suggested the principles which a policy and process of assessment should fulfil. We emphasised the need for objective assessment in the arts and proposed four main areas for assessment — creative, technical, critical and contextual — and seven related learning objectives. Finally we proposed four principles of progression which an effective arts education should aim to promote for all pupils from 5 to 16.

Chapter seven

DEVELOPING THE ARTS IN SCHOOLS

PRINCIPLES AND PRIORITIES

178. In this book we have argued that a new framework is needed for the development of the arts in schools. It is one that takes full account of contemporary developments in education as a whole, in arts education in particular, and also in the arts outside schools. Such a framework should provide a common language and points of reference for curriculum planning, teaching and assessment in all of the arts and across the 5-16 age range. The framework elaborated here recognises the need for a cross-cultural conception of the arts, both logically, given the complexities of definition, and educationally, given the pressing need for forms of teaching and learning which take proper account of cultural diversity.

179. We have argued that the arts should be planned for collectively as a generic area of the curriculum. Provision should be related to a number of distinctive modes of understanding — visual, aural, kinaesthetic, verbal and enactive — and should recognise both the different opportunities that each of these offers all pupils, and the eventual need for specialisation. A shift is needed in the teaching of the arts towards a conception of cultural education based on a dynamic relationship between pupils' own creative work and their critical understanding of existing work and cultural practices.

180. We identified making and appraising as the two principal ways of engaging in the arts and described them in terms of several related processes: exploring, forming, performing, presenting, responding and evaluating. Making and appraising form the first axis of our framework. The second axis consists of four main elements of learning: concepts, skills, attitudes and values, and information. The framework is intended as a guide for planning courses, and also for tackling the complex issues of progression and assessment. We identified the key principles of progression and assessment and seven general learning objectives which can be used as a basis for more specific objectives within different arts specialisms.

181. We have been principally concerned with the arts in the formal curriculum. The measure of a school is not only the curriculum it publishes but 'the quality of relationships, the concern for equality of opportunity, the values exemplified in the way the school sets about its task and the ways in which it is organised and managed' (DES 1985b).

Balanced provision for the arts can enliven the whole ethos of the school and promote the sense of purpose and belonging which is needed to motivate pupils and teachers alike to successful work across the curriculum.

PRACTICE AND INNOVATION

182.   Curriculum development has to be guided by policy, and the arguments we have developed here may provide schools with the basis of such a policy. But policies also need to be implemented. The work of the Arts in Schools project was directed at giving schools practical support in developing the arts in the curriculum. Our approach was based on three assumptions about effective curriculum development.

(a) *Local needs*
  The arguments which have been presented in this book are intended to apply to policies for the arts in all schools. Practical development has to take account of the specific circumstances, interests and resources of individual schools.

(b) *Staff development*
  Innovations in the curriculum cannot be carried forward effectively without the support, enthusiasm and understanding of the teachers concerned. The most effective curriculum development is where staff are actively involved in planning the initiatives, and can see the benefits to their own work.

(c) *Institutional support*
  Curriculum initiatives need the support of the school as a whole and a commitment to the necessary resources and facilities.

On this basis, there are a number of stages in the development and implementation of a school's arts policy. These include the four enumerated below.

1. Curriculum review

183.   The first step is to establish what the current provision for the arts is in the school, and to identify areas of need. The information required includes:

- the range of arts disciplines taught;
- numbers of staff involved;
- the time given to learning *in* and learning *through* the arts;
- the available resources and budget;
- the styles and content of teaching;
- methods of record-keeping and assessment.

2. Developing the policy

184.   Using this information, the existing provision can be evaluated in terms of the principles of provision discussed in previous chapters. The next step is to initiate discussions with staff and with governors about the form of provision that is needed in the school. The policy being developed should address each element of the review. This process should relate the arts to the school's whole-curriculum policy, and take careful account of the statutory requirements of the National Curriculum.

3. Staff development

185.   In order to implement the policy, it will usually be necessary to devise strategies for staff development. The most common strategies used within the project were:

School-based
- professional days for the staff of primary schools or the specialist arts teachers in secondary schools;
- artists in residence;
- visits to and from specialist teachers and pupils from other schools;
- in-school support by the LEA advisory service;

Out of school
- teachers' cross-phase and cross-arts development groups;
- teacher exchanges;
- arts festivals;
- joint performances and workshops;
- visiting arts venues for performances, exhibitions etc.;
- conferences, lectures etc.

It is not always necessary to bring in specialist expertise. Teachers often have skills and knowledge which are not used in the day-to-day work and organisation of the school. Collaboration between the teachers in the school can often generate mutual in-service sessions.

4. Developing resources

186. It is vital to organise the resources of time, space and facilities appropriately for the different arts disciplines. The performing arts will need extra time and space. Ideally these spaces should be sound-proofed, or at a suitable distance from quiet study areas. Each discipline needs its own support; all can benefit from making full use of the resources in the wider community, including:

- local arts venues — galleries, theatres, community centres, concert halls;
- national drama, dance and opera companies, music ensembles, film and media organisations;
- local artists and craftspeople.

Detailed accounts of these various stages and approaches to curriculum development in the arts are given in our related publication, *The Arts 5-16: Practice and Innovation*. Detailed suggestions and resources for a structured programme of staff development are given in our third allied publication, *The Arts 5-16: A Workpack for Teachers*. Together these three publications are intended to give schools access to ideas and strategies for a whole-hearted and concerted provision for the arts in the curriculum.

187. We began this book by emphasising the need for curriculum development in the arts to be guided in schools by a coherent policy. The experience of the Arts in Schools project is that where the arts are well provided for, the whole school benefits in atmosphere and motivation. These benefits do not arise by accident. They come from a recognition that the arts have essential roles in education both in themselves and in concert with other disciplines, in fulfilling the aims of a broad and balanced curriculum; they come from a creative and determined effort to achieve this balance, not only in a statement of aims, but in the daily practice of the arts in schools.

Appendix: the Arts in Schools project, 1985-89

In 1982 the Calouste Gulbenkian Foundation published the report of a national committee of inquiry, *The Arts in Schools: Principles, Practice and Provision*. The report argued that all of the arts have essential roles in the education of all pupils in primary and secondary schools. It also found that in too many schools arts provision is inadequate and needs urgent improvement. The arguments and recommendations of this report were applauded by LEAs and firmly endorsed by the Department of Education and Science. In September 1985, with the support of many LEAs and arts organisations, the School Curriculum Development Committee established the Arts in Schools project as a major initiative '*to give practical support to teachers, schools and local authorities to improve education in and through the arts for all young people*'. The detailed brief of the project was developed at a national seminar of teachers, advisers, teacher educators and arts organisations.

The aims of the project were:

1. to identify constraints on the arts in schools and practical ways of overcoming them;
2. to enable teachers to develop curriculum initiatives in the arts;
3. to document, analyse and disseminate examples of valued practice;
4. to publish curriculum guidelines;
5. to increase public and professional awareness of the roles of the arts in education.

The project was concerned with all of the arts and with the whole 5-16 age range and was organised in partnership with eighteen LEAs in England and Wales. Each authority appointed a full-time co-ordinator to work in consultation with the project's central team, and convened a development group of teachers from primary and secondary schools to plan, carry out and document practical work in schools. The project involved more than five hundred teachers, headteachers, advisers and professional artists and generated practical curriculum initiatives in over two hundred schools.

The central project team

Director
Dr Ken Robinson

Project Officers
Gillian Wills (1985-86)
Dave Allen (1985-88)
Jill Henderson (1986-89)
Phil Everitt (1988-89)

Information Officer
Mike Cahill (1986-89)

Administrator
Andrew Worsdale

Administrative Officers
Kathy Bradley (1986-87)
Catrina Edmondson (1987-88)
Helen Bradbear (1988-89)

Members of the monitoring group

John Tomlinson (Chair)	Professor and Director, University of Warwick Institute of Education
Glennis Andrews	Deputy Head, Tyldesley County Primary School, Wigan
Madhu Anjali	Assistant Education Officer, Berkshire
Godfrey Brandt	Senior Education Officer, Arts Council of Great Britain
Helen Carter	Professional Officer, National Curriculum Council
Robert Fowler	Principal, Central School of Speech and Drama
Daphne Gould (from 1988)	Headteacher, Mulberry School for Girls, ILEA and Member, National Curriculum Council
Dr David Hargreaves	Chief Inspector, Inner London Education Authority
Dr Seamus Hegarty	Deputy Director, National Foundation for Educational Research
Pat Martin	Head of Drama, Stratford upon Avon High School, Warwickshire
Robin Peverett	Headteacher, Dulwich College Preparatory School, Kent
Sue Robertson	Director of Education Programmes, South Bank Centre
Julian Watson (to 1986)	Headteacher, Castlecroft Primary School, Wolverhampton
Roger Williams (from 1986)	HMI

(Posts are those held during the lifetime of the project.)

Project co-ordinators

In its development phase (1985-88), the Arts in Schools project involved partnerships with groups of teachers in eighteen local education authorities. The co-ordinators of these groups were as follows:

BERKSHIRE
Hamish Preston
Veronica Treacher

CLWYD
Mike Evans

DEVON
Shirley Page
Keith Rattray

EAST SUSSEX
Phil Everitt

ESSEX
Colin Humphreys

HAMPSHIRE
Jack Brook

HARROW
Jill Heller

HUMBERSIDE AND
LINCOLNSHIRE
Gordon Beastall
Christine Humphrey
Jillian Lewis

ILEA
David Sheppard

KENT
Maggie Anwell

LEICESTERSHIRE
Jim Dutton

NORTHUMBERLAND
Tony Murray
Clive Wright

NORTH YORKSHIRE
Sally Hull
Brian Sellors

OXFORDSHIRE
Michael Knightall
David Menday
Bridie Sullivan

SHROPSHIRE
Janet Bacon
Roger Turner

WEST GLAMORGAN
Margaret Phillips

WIGAN
Glennis Andrews
Dennis Lavelle
Bob Mason

References

Abbs, P. (1982) *English Within the Arts: A Radical Alternative for English and the Arts in the Curriculum,* Hodder and Stoughton.

Abbs, P. (1989) 'Tactful approach to life', *Times Higher Education Supplement,* 10 January 1989.

Arts in Schools project team (1990a) *The Arts 5-16: Practice and Innovation,* Oliver & Boyd.

Arts in Schools project team (1990b) *The Arts 5-16: A Workpack for Teachers,* Oliver & Boyd.

Aspin, D. (1984) *Objectivity and Assessment in the Arts: The Problem of Aesthetic Education,* National Association for Education in the Arts.

Benjamin, W. (1977) 'The work of art in the age of mechanical reproduction' in Curran, J. et al. *Mass Communication and Society,* Edward Arnold.

Best, D. (1984) 'The Dangers of "Aesthetic Education"', *Oxford Review of Education,* Vol. 10, No. 2, pp.159-167.

Best, D. (1985) *Feeling and Reason in the Arts,* George Allen & Unwin.

Blacking, J. (1982) 'A Case for Higher Education in the Arts' in: Robinson, K. (ed.), *The Arts and Higher Education,* SRHE/Leverhulme.

Bolton, G. (1980) *Towards a Theory of Drama in Education,* Longman.

British Film Institute (1989) *Primary Media Education: A Curriculum Statement,* BFI.

Bruner, J. (1966) *Toward a Theory of Instruction,* Harvard University Press.

Calouste Gulbenkian Foundation (1982) *The Arts in Schools: Principles, Practice and Provision,* Gulbenkian Foundation.

Cleave, S. and Sharpe, C. (1986) *The Arts: A Preparation to Teach,* National Foundation for Educational Research.

Crafts Council (1987) *Response to the DES Consultative Document on the National Curriculum.*

DES and the Welsh Office (1978) *Primary Education in England,* HMSO.

DES and the Welsh Office (1981) *Aesthetic Development: A Report from the Assessment of Performance Unit Exploratory Group on Aesthetic Development,* HMSO.

DES and the Welsh Office (1983) *Popular Television and Schoolchildren,* HMSO.

DES and the Welsh Office (1985a) *Better Schools,* HMSO.

DES and the Welsh Office (1985b) *The Curriculum from 5 to 16: Curriculum Matters,* HMSO.

DES and the Welsh Office (1985c) *Education for All,* Comnd 9453, HMSO.

DES and the Welsh Office (1987) *National Curriculum: Task Group on Assessment and Testing: A Report,* HMSO.

DES and the Welsh Office (1988) *The Curriculum from 5 to 16: The Responses to Curriculum Matters 2,* HMSO.

DES and the Welsh Office (1989a) *Design and Technology for ages 5-16,* HMSO.

DES and the Welsh Office (1989b) *English for Ages 5-16,* HMSO.

DES and the Welsh Office (1989c) *National Curriculum: History Working Group Interim Report,* HMSO.

DES and the Welsh Office (1989d) *The National Curriculum: From*

Policy to Practice, HMSO.

1988 Education Reform Act. Chapter 40. HMSO.

Grotowski, J. (1968) *Towards A Poor Theatre,* Eyre Methuen.

Hansard, 5 April 1982, Vol. 21, HMSO.

Hargreaves, D. (1982) *The Challenge for the Comprehensive School: Culture, Curriculum and Community,* Routledge and Kegan Paul.

Hornbrook, D. (1989) *Education and Dramatic Art,* Blackwell.

House of Commons, Education, Science and Arts committee (1981-82) 8th Report, HC49.

Kelly, G. A. (1963) *A Theory of Personality: The Psychology of Personal Constructs,* New York: W.W. Norton.

Kuhn, T. S. (1970) *The Structure of Scientific Revolutions,* Chicago University Press.

Music Advisers National Association (1986) *Assessment and Progression in Music Education,* MANA.

Myerscough, J. (1988) *The Economic Importance of the Arts in Britain,* Policy Studies Institute.

National Association for Education in the Arts (1987) *The National Curriculum: Implications for the Arts,* NAEA.

O'Grady, C. (1989) 'Crafts at the Crossroads', *Times Educational Supplement,* 18 November 1988.

Osborne, H. (1985) 'The Aesthetic in Education and in Life' in Ross, M. (ed.), *The Aesthetic in Education,* Pergamon.

Owusu, K. (1986) *The Struggle for Black Arts in Britain,* Comedia.

Pick, J. (1986) *Managing the Arts: The British Experience,* Rheingold.

Polanyi, M. (1969) *Personal Knowledge,* Routledge and Kegan Paul.

Popper, K. (1969) *Conjectures and Refutations: The Growth of Scientific Knowledge,* Routledge and Kegan Paul.

Read, H. (1945) *Education Through Art,* Faber and Faber.

Reid, L. A. (1969) *Meaning in the Arts,* George Allen & Unwin.

Richardson, M. (1948) *Art and the Child,* University of London Press.

Ross, M. (1978) *The Creative Arts,* Heinemann.

Ross, M. (ed.) (1985) *The Aesthetic in Education,* Pergamon.

Slade, P. (1954) *Child Drama,* University of London.

Swanwick, K. (1979) *A Basis for Music Education,* NFER/Nelson.

Swanwick, K. (1989) *Music, Mind and Education,* Routledge and Kegan Paul.

Taylor, R. (1986) *Educating for Art,* Longman.

Van Santen, J. (1988) 'Art Education and Cultural Experience' in *Artists in Education,* Commonwealth Institute.

Viola, W. (1936) *Child Art and Franz Cizek,* Vienna: Austrian Red Cross.

Wagner, B. J. (1979) *Dorothy Heathcote: Drama as an Educational Medium,* Hutchinson.

Williams, R. (1971) *The Long Revolution,* Penguin.

Witkin, R. (1974) *The Intelligence of Feeling,* Heinemann.

Worpole, K. (1989) *Magic and Transformation: A View of the Arts in the South,* Southern Arts.

Young, J. Z. (1951) *Doubt and Certainty in Science: A Biologist's Reflections on the Brain,* Reith Lectures, BBC Publications.

Index